Letting Go of Jason

Letting Go of Jason

✦

A Young Man with Asperger's Syndrome and Bipolar Disorder

Connie Aull

iUniverse, Inc.
New York Lincoln Shanghai

Letting Go of Jason
A Young Man with Asperger's Syndrome and Bipolar Disorder

iUniverse books may be ordered through booksellers or by contacting:

iUniverse
2021 Pine Lake Road, Suite 100
Lincoln, NE 68512
www.iuniverse.com
1-800-Authors (1-800-288-4677)

Most names and places have been changed.

ISBN: 0-595-34213-2

Printed in the United States of America

This book is dedicated to my mother, Geraldine Keef Moreland, who taught me about the power of unconditional love and believing in myself.

Contents

Foreword

So many people have encouraged, prayed and hoped for and with our family. Life has not been easy, but amidst times of distress there were signs of hope to get us through. I want to spend this time with others who have Asperger's Syndrome children who struggle with depression. I want to encourage you by sharing Jason's life story to let you know you are not alone. I hope I pass along to you a little knowledge of Asperger's Syndrome and bipolar disorder and a little cheer as you read about our lives. Letting go of Jason was a long, hard process that taught me how precious life really is. It also taught me that God provides me with the strength to let go, so Jason can have the freedom to live his own life. We all have family, friends and significant others that we must release. I hope my book helps you to let go.

Acknowledgements

Along the way there have been a few special teachers and public administrators of various agencies that took extra time to learn about Asperger's and about Jason. They knew the cracks and yet fought to mend them for Jason's sake. I would like to personally thank them. Reverend Turner, the Staff at Forest Heights Lodge, Mr. Tom Parmalee, DDSN Director of Operations, Rufuss Britt III, Mr. Bagwell and Bill Trezza. A special thanks to Joan Bozzone and Pat Cook for editing my book.

Thank you to my husband, John, for always being there for me. Thanks to my family for always being willing to listen. Thank you, my friends, for giving me sound counsel and believing in me when times were tough. Jason and Luke, thank you for making a difference in my life. Thank you, God, for your sustaining, unconditional love.

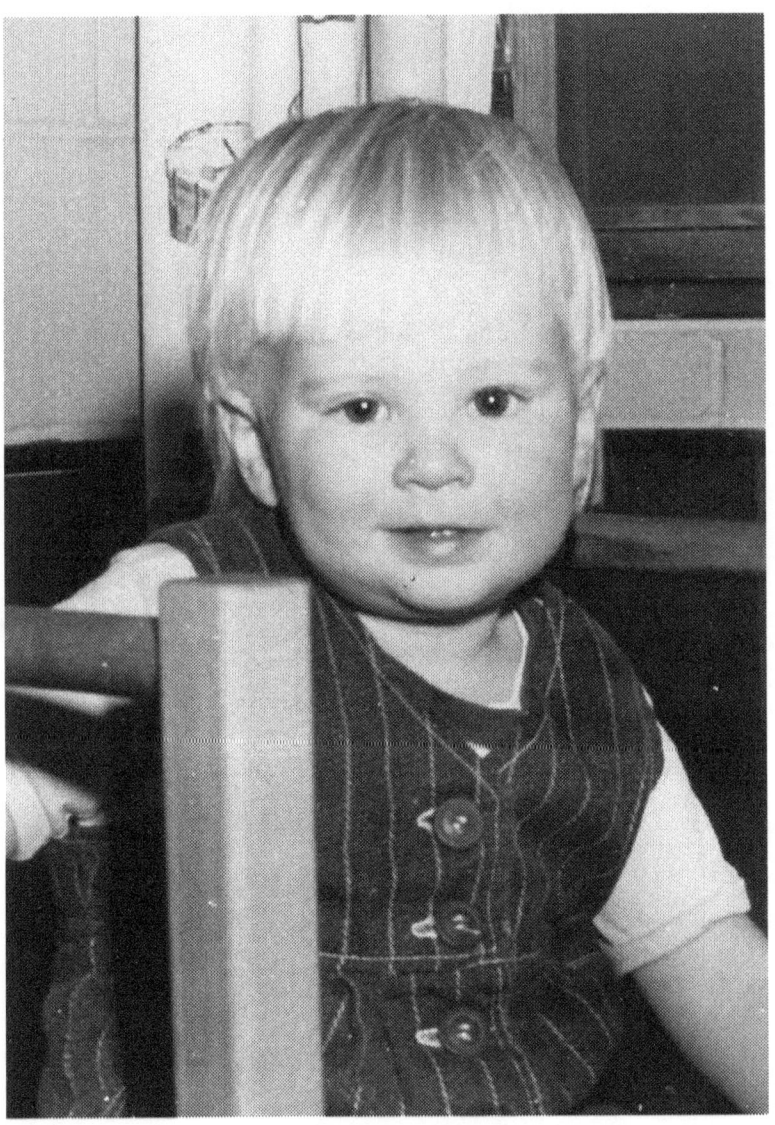

Jason 18 months old

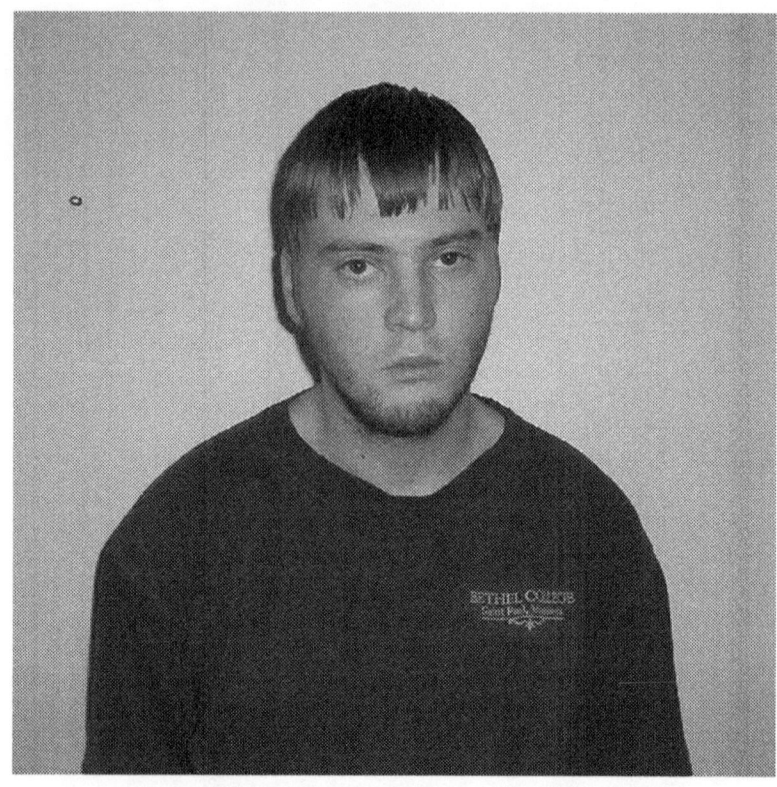

Jason at age 24

I

The Journey Begins

I was overjoyed with the miracle that grew inside of me. It was my first-born. I was amazed at the wonder and awe of the nine months it took for a child to be born. I was trusting and believing that my child would be healthy and strong and would grow up to make a difference in this world. I wanted my child to be different, to make a special mark in this world of ours. I dreamed of the time when he would walk, talk, and then one day, become independent. I looked forward to the opportunity to teach my child about life and then one day, to let him go. Having a child is one step in the long, hard process of letting go that parents all must go through. I hoped I was ready for the journey.

After 24 hours of hard labor, my husband, John, and I were full of joy when our first son, Jason, was born on April 22, 1980, in Brevard, North Carolina. He was truly a beautiful baby. He was easy to care for. He rarely cried and loved to lie in his crib and sing melodies to himself. As an infant, Jason would lie in one place all day long and just look around. When he began to crawl, I remember him scooting around like a turtle. I had a job cleaning houses, and Jason would sit in his chair contently all day as long as he was fed and changed. He was my first-born, so I just thought I had a very good baby boy.

When Jason was nineteen months old, his brother, Luke, was born on November 30, 1981. Luke was a handsome baby with such a grand disposition. He lit up our lives each time he had a smile on his face. He was a special child born with bi-lateral cleft palate, also known as harelip. Unfortunately, many surgeries were needed to repair his birth defect. At three months old, Luke had his first surgery on half of his lip. When he was six months old, the doctors were able to complete the other half of his lip. The doctors rebuilt Luke's palate at eighteen months, and he was able to suck for the first time in his life. Despite the scars and the pain, Luke was a trooper. What joy this child brought into our lives! His life has shown us the truth that there is joy amidst pain. I was so pleased that Jason had a brother. Jason had to be careful with his brother. He was not allowed to touch Luke's face, and had to learn great self-control to protect his little brother.

During the special times with Luke at the hospital, Jason stayed with a friend named Joyce. She brought love and joy to Jason's life. My family lived far away, so Joyce became a part of our family. It was so important to have a friend when times were hard, someone with whom we could share the tears and laughter. She was a special person who was there for me when the road was really rough. Joyce was there for all of us, but mostly for Jason. He became very close to her.

When Jason was 20 months old, he became sick. He couldn't keep anything down and had chronic diarrhea. He quickly became dehydrated. The doctors hospitalized him for a week. He recovered from looking lethargic to being his happy old self. We were concerned about his digestive system, when at two years, he once again became dehydrated. The doctors hospitalized him again and placed him on a special diet. He could eat only rice products and oats, and drink soy milk. For six months the doctor slowly added items to his diet, but Jason continued to struggle when we added meat and fruits.

Unfortunately, at 30 months old, Jason became sick again, and this time he was hospitalized for ten days. The doctors were so concerned that they sent us to a specialist. The specialist was troubled over the lack of fat in his diet. He put him on a high protein diet. We took him home and slowly introduced chicken soup, beef broth, and fruits to his diet. Jason began to do very well and successfully healed over three months time. He was well-behaved the entire time he was sick with what had been diagnosed as gastroenteritis. He was content to eat whatever we gave him. We continued to wonder how such a small child could be so content. Over the one year of sickness, it was still so easy to take care of our son.

During this time, Luke had had three surgeries, and Jason was finally healing when I developed depression. My body was so tired all the time, and I needed help with the boys. With my family so far away, the only person available locally was Joyce. One day, I woke up and just could not get out of bed. I called Joyce, and she came to get the boys. I called the doctor. The doctor chose for me to go to a special psychiatric hospital nearby where I could get help. They took many blood tests and screened me for depression. I told the doctors that I remembered having depression when I was thirteen, sixteen, and nineteen years old. I was afraid to tell anyone, and the depressive episodes lasted one to two months.

The doctor at the hospital sent me home after a week. My sister came to help with the boys while I rested and waited for blood test results. The results came back, and I was totally unprepared when the doctor explained to me that I had bipolar disorder. Bipolar disorder is an inherited chemical imbalance in the brain and is a "manic depressive illness which tends to be cyclical, with periods of elated overactivity (mania) irregularly alternating with deep depression. Periods of normality, sandwiched between the extremes, may last a short time or years."[1] He placed me on lithium, a medication used to treat bipolar disorder patients, and rest for three weeks until my energy came back. I was not interested in knowing anything about what I had, just that I could get better over time. In about four weeks, I was doing very well, and it seemed lithium was a cure.

I was 23 years old, young and impulsive. Luke's surgeries and Jason's illness were a constant stress. Taking care of two healthy children is hard enough, much less two children with special needs. I was thankful that Jason was getting well, and Luke's cleft palate was healing nicely. I felt so angry when people said, "Isn't it wonderful what doctors can do these days?" Yes, it was wonderful, but think about living with Luke's condition day after day, and feeding him with a syringe every 45 minutes. Sometimes, the best thing to do is to say nothing, just help the person who is struggling. Thankfully, the lithium really helped me to have a healthier perspective on life.

2

The Symptoms

When Jason was three years old, I went to work, and he and Luke attended the local daycare center. The daycare workers noticed that he did not play with the other children. He was so much fun to play with one-on-one, but he withdrew when there were others around him to play. I remember vividly at the age of four, Jason lying on his bed and reciting the biblical poems that he had heard on the tapes in the car. We realized then that he was gifted with an exceptional memory. He liked to build symmetrical legos that were color schemed before he even learned the names of colors. He did not want to tear down what he built. However, he took apart our clocks, radios, and anything of interest, but never put them together again. He seemed to enjoy being alone. He bonded well with adults one-on-one, but with children, he remained aloof.

In kindergarten, we learned that Jason was struggling to keep up with his work and was not socializing with the other children on the playground. The teacher wanted us to test him to see if he had Attention Deficit Disorder (ADD). ADD is described as "a behavioral syndrome characterized by inattention and distractibility, restlessness, inability to sit still, and difficulty concentrating on one thing for any period of time."[2] Jason was having trouble with organization and concentration in the classroom. The public school systems psychologist tested him and concluded that he was very imaginative. They suggested that a private school setting would be best to help him. We chose to put him in private school. However, the problems of not playing with his peers and struggling with kindergarten skills began to cause us concern.

Structure was so important that he lived and breathed it. For example, we lived in one house in South Carolina for fifteen years. Jason was four years old when we moved to this house and attended a private kindergarten. In five-year-old kindergarten he started having homework assignments. From the very beginning, we could not easily motivate him to complete homework. If he did not have interest in the subject, he had no motivation to complete the smallest of assignments.

After school each day, Jason had chores around the house. This provided him with an allowance which, in turn, gave him the delight of buying his one or two half-pints of chocolate ice cream every Wednesday. Each Wednesday at 4 p.m., the ice cream man's truck came singing down our driveway. Jason dropped his homework, darted for his allowance, and dashed out the front door to meet the ice cream man. He always added to his collection of chocolate ice cream, which took the entire bottom drawer of the freezer. He tried hard to eat the ice cream but he always bought more than he could consume.

It was common for us to tutor Jason every day or at least put his assignments on a time table, so we could keep him organized as he struggled to get his homework done. One afternoon as I tutored him, he was preoccupied and worked slowly. I could not get him to do his homework no matter what I did. Finally, out of frustration, I asked him, "What is going on today that you refuse to do your math?" Jason began to cry as he said, "The ice cream man is late and is not coming. I do not want to work without him. I expected him. Remember Mom? It is Wednesday. Can't we call him?" Even when Jason was seventeen years old, he counted on the ice cream man like a dog waiting for a bone.

Remember there are important issues, people, and schedules in the life of Asperger's Syndrome children. We needed to keep a schedule as much as possible especially for Jason. An Asperger's child requires structure to help him deal with life. He must know where he lives and where things are stored in his bedroom. He is obsessive about such matters. An Asperger's child learns by observation. He changes step-by-step. He has his own timetable, which takes patience and memory for the parents. The ice cream man is not just anyone, but a part of his life. What seems so trivial to us can be a mountain to climb for him.

When Jason turned six, problems with high anxiety and fears became a part of his life. We noticed symptoms of these fears when he was an infant. As a baby he loved water. Then, one day he became afraid of it. He started to walk when he was one year old, then just sat down and did not attempt to walk again until he was nineteen months old. When he tried to ride a bike, he became overwhelmingly afraid of it. When his brother Luke began to ride, Jason overcame the fears he had. At age eight, he succeeded. At this age, he also overcame his fear of swimming. Another example of his high anxiety occurred when he found a mosquito in the house. He ran to his bedroom, climbed into bed, covered up his whole body except his nose, and stated, "The mosquitoes are going to drink my blood. They're everywhere."

We could not understand why he had all the fears and anxiety. We were frustrated by not knowing how to deal with these emotions. Often we were afraid to discipline him because we were concerned that we might make matters worse. Calming him during these fearful episodes was not easy and took a lot of time and patience. The symptoms for Asperger's were all there: the need for structure and routine, the desire to be alone, and the unrealistic fears and anxieties. But no doctor had diagnosed him yet. I would often just watch Jason as he spent time in a dream world, yet we could not put our finger on what was wrong. We needed help in determining what the problem was and how to best help Jason.

3

Essence of Time

We pushed hard because we wanted Jason to get outside and enjoy himself. His brother, his neighbors, and John and I all tried to prompt and encourage Jason to go out and play. He spent almost all of his time in his room or watching the Discovery Channel. He had to be coaxed to go out, given an incentive of some kind, and sometimes flat-out bribed. "You go out and play, and we can have ice cream later," or "You go out and play now, and later you can watch your favorite TV show." We tried anything we could think of to get him out in the fresh air.

One day he ran to the door, slammed it shut, bolted it and yelled, "They're coming!" I looked out to see, and there were the neighborhood boys coming to ask Luke and Jason to play ball. He almost acted like they were aliens coming to get him. I tried to convince him to go out, to no avail. Some days we succeeded, and other times, going out to play was a lost cause. He excused himself when he said, "I'm too tired", or "I just don't want to."

We wanted so much for him to just be a boy and relax, enjoy life separate from reading, studying, attending school, or being in his room. Balance is what we were hoping for. Nothing ever consistently worked to teach him to balance his time between his homework, school, and play. Jason just enjoyed being alone, concentrating on things that were important to him. When something sparked his interest, he would obsessively pursue it. I often wondered how we could get him obsessive over exercise. He was clumsy in playing sports. He had no interest in them. We did get him to play T-ball, but when the hard ball was used, Jason quit.

When he did go out and play what a joy it was to my heart watching him run and smile, playing with the neighbors or his brother. Jason was tall and slender, so basketball was easy for him to play, but he got no pleasure from it and didn't pursue it. We built a swimming pool so all the neighbors would come to our house and swim. He only came out to swim when we earnestly pursued him. John and I tried to make everything available to the boys, including Jason's favorite outside activity, which was jumping on the trampoline. He would jump and jump until he was worn out. Then, he would lay across the mat soaking in the sun, carefree and happy. Happy! There are not many times I could say that word, but Jason was happy and content in that one moment in time.

He just wanted to learn and do everything on his own timetable. Time was only an issue when Jason made it one. There were two types of time, in my opinion, that seemed to exist in his life. One was when I had to get something that Jason wanted NOW! He did not understand any delay. The discussion at hand could not wait. He was confused, and he needed the matter to be put in order right away, so he would not be full of anxiety. Our goal was to calm that anxiety.

Then, there were some points in our lives when time seemed nonexistent to Jason. The world went on whether he chose to make decisions or not. Life could pass Jason by when it came to chores, school, or whatever. He believed it would all just happen when it was meant to be. We, on the other hand, believed it was important for Jason to develop some self-motivation.

Whatever the task, it would get done once he put his mind to it. I could pray, prod, threaten, yell, stomp out of a room, or cry, but it would not have the impact of motivating him. If I gave reasons, either he didn't understand, or he didn't care. Ambivalence toward time is a good way to express this situation. When he was ready, he believed time would be ready for him. Otherwise, time seemed to fade away in his mind.

Jason has always taken the time to obey the rules. This is one of his greatest attributes. Thank goodness he has always found it important in life to tell the truth. Rules are important to him, and they have to be obeyed. He has never broken anyone's rules intentionally because he lives by them. For example, it is a rule to tell the truth, so Jason always takes the time to tell the truth as he sees it. If you ask him how he feels, he always says, "Half this, half that," or just "OK" because in one day he has many feelings. Yet, he still tends to be confused regarding what feelings are. To avoid telling a lie, he will not give a direct, clear answer. No matter what he does, Jason makes sure the truth prevails.

When he was six, we took him for tests at a medical facility in Georgia because his anxieties had increased. Their tests concluded that Jason had depression and possible ADD. Medication was suggested for the depression, but we felt that giving him medication could be dangerous at his age, so we decided to wait to see if the symptoms worsened. Depression is "a psychoneurotic or psychotic disorder marked especially by sadness, inactivity, difficulty in thinking and concentration, a significant increase or decrease in appetite and time spent sleeping, feelings of dejection and hopelessness, and sometimes suicidal tendencies."[3] The doctors gave us this possible diagnosis with no treatment suggestions other than medication. We struggled daily to understand what was wrong. We felt like even the doctors were not specific enough in explaining what depression meant…especially in a child. The fact remained that we were left with the responsibility of how to best help Jason. We did not know how a young boy could get depressed, much less how to help him get better. We just assumed that his fears and anxieties must be symptoms of depression. Our frustrations over the unknown continued as he got older.

4

Homework

Jason continued to have problems daily. We structured the household activities more and developed a checkmark system to keep up with chores and homework. John and I alternated days in assisting him with his homework. It was a long, hard task each afternoon to get him to do his work. Taking turns tutoring him with his homework assignments gave us a little break.

After an assignment was given along with the deadline, the war over homework would begin as soon as Jason entered the house. Even if it was only to write a paragraph, a one hour homework assignment to some meant two to three hours of homework for Jason and us. Our assistance was always needed in order for the homework to be completed. Writing about feelings was like torture to him, because they were not concrete but were abstract in nature. When it was complete, he felt that it was not right or exactly like he wanted it to be, so he would start again. I knew he would do it again and again if I left the homework completely up to him. Many times the work just did not get turned in.

Everything was black or white in his mind, and Jason's rules were rules we had to learn.

Jason's head-to-hand coordination slowed his thought processes, so he could not keep up with what he wanted to say. He often repeated what had been said to him, a condition called echolalia. He would become frustrated, and these frustrations led to a lack of motivation. He spent a lot of time searching meticulously for the right word, so a sentence would say exactly what he had in his mind. We found that verbal testing in school helped so much, and would save us and the teachers many headaches. Everything just needed to be perfect in Jason's world.

We purchased a "Dragon Dictate" software program to help Jason be able to do his English assignments. Thank God for high technology! It allowed someone to speak into the computer, instead of having to type. It worked, but we struggled to get him to use it. Unfortunately, even with the "Dragon Dictate" he was slow. His frustration continued no matter how hard we tried. He slapped his head with his hands when he became frustrated with his work. Jason struggled to get the right words down on paper. When he did, they were never the right words he wanted, so he felt driven to begin again. I was worn out by the end of the day just trying to help him help himself. His anxiety grew worse, and he continued to have difficulty making friends. He spent a lot of time alone in the bathroom as he got older, talking to himself and doing his homework. He was diligent and wanted everything flawless, which added to his frustrations. Jason was so kind, creative, and loving that it broke our hearts to see him suffer just to do his homework assignments. I felt sorry for him, because upon coming home from school, getting a snack, off he had to go to get his homework done. Even if I gave him some "down time," the homework was inevitable. I even tried rewards when the homework was complete, but that did not help.

I was so relieved when homework was over each day. I thought, "Ahhh! What a relief, homework is over for today! I made it through without tears or running into my bedroom sobbing for relief from the chore of helping my son with his homework." He tried so hard, and yet, it took him so long to do even one problem in math. In math, he felt compelled to do the problems just right, or it was not good enough for him. He did not do math the way you or

I would tackle it. He did math inside out, instead of left to right. He already knew the answers, and he wanted to know why he couldn't put them down and be over with it. No, the teacher wanted math done in steps and wanted to see his work. Then, she wanted so many problems to be done, and they were all essentially the same. Jason was only interested in the theories of math. He would spend hours working on a math theory to present to his teachers. The teachers loved his theories, and often asked him to share them with the class.

An Individualized Education Plan (IEP) is a specialized plan which describes the student's goals and objectives that a team sets for that student for a school year. Working with his teacher, I fixed his IEP, so that he only had to do three or four of the same type of math problems, instead of eight to ten like the rest of the class. This helped, but he still struggled to get his math completed. Some days he was just so slow. I sat beside him lovingly trying to encourage him and direct him to stay focused on his problems. I left him for a few minutes with the goal for him to do a problem in ten minutes. Often, I came back to find him staring off into space. Instead of working the problem out on paper, he was calculating the answer, so he could then write the process of how he got the answer. Oh, how I wished sometimes that days could be normal! But what was normal? I surely didn't know anymore.

Summers were such relief for my husband and me. During the school year we took turns with homework, thinking that the stress would be less, but it wasn't. When John helped, I sat back and prayed, hoping the day went well, so Jason could have time to go out and play for a short while. The days of homework seemed to never end, and with each year, it got harder. Many times we took a deep breath and entered his room again to help him get through the day. If the homework did not get completed, then it just didn't.

When the day was over, I could say to myself, "I tried my best, and thank you, God, that the homework is over."

5

Pieces of the Puzzle

Despite structuring his life and working with Jason to teach him organization on a daily basis, he continued to have problems with anxiety, stress, and organization. We worked with him daily by going over each day's plans in the morning and then again in the afternoon when he came home from school. We also gave Jason a watch to help him keep up with time. Jason and his watch were inseparable. These things seemed to lessen his anxiety levels.

Part of his stress came from his lack of social skills. He was alienated from his peers. He recently said he had felt like he was like Rudolph the red-nosed reindeer. He felt isolated because the children did not include him in their games. From second to fourth grade, Jason said he just did not know how to talk to people. Jason had this feeling that they had something that he didn't have. They had the ability to pick up social cues by being around people and learning their ways. Oh, how difficult it must have been for him! I was often sad that Jason had no friends; however, it seemed he preferred to be alone. I desperately wanted him to have friends.

Teachers were an important part of his life. If the teacher was well-disciplined and structured, Jason often did well. I wondered what the teachers were going through with him from day-to-day. Dear, dear teachers, how I sympathized with their struggles with a classroom of 30 very diversified children who were eager to learn! Then, there was student number 31. His name was Jason. He sat quietly in the back of the room disorganized and confused. He did not interact unless interaction was initiated by another. He did not act out or create any disturbances. He was bright, but slow. "Jason we are on page twenty. Twenty Jason!" the teacher repeated. She thought maybe he couldn't hear, but he heard everything else. "Your child possibly has ADD" the teacher suggested. Therefore, we worked on how to make his classes appropriate to his skill level, to reduce frustrations.

Jason's fifth grade teacher loved teaching, which helped him to be more motivated than ever. She was so creative that he actually had less homework than any other year before or since. "If only all teachers were like that for him," I thought. He continued having problems with organization, but other than that, it was a successful school year. His disorganization meant he lost his school papers or he did not know his homework assignments. He was frustrated and confused, and at some points he felt overwhelmed by anxiety that continued day after day. He did show creativity that the teachers observed and found fascinating.

One day in fifth grade, Jason went to catch the bus. He had a special book he was interested in reading. He realized after fifteen minutes that he had missed the bus. He didn't want to go to school or home. So, he decided to sit down in the grass a few feet from a busy street to read his book. The bus was not important to him, and nothing distracted him, not even the cars going by as neighbors took their children to school. Somehow, for hours he remained on that grass oblivious to his surroundings. Jason was enthralled with this book, possibly trying to desperately finish what he had started. Many times, closure had to take place on tasks he was involved in, before he could go on to the next step in his day.

The bus time was 7:30 a.m., and at 11:00 a.m. I received a knock at my door. The Vice-Principal from the elementary school knew Jason, saw him on the side of the road, and kindly chose to pick him up and bring him home. She then volunteered to take him to school for me. I knew he would not go with strangers, but he could have been hurt on that busy road. I felt helpless and never in control of what happened to Jason on any day. Everything felt like life was on a slow pendulum, and waiting was not my greatest strength. The key was that I had to release control in order to benefit our special son and myself. His timetable always stemmed from overcoming some type of fear or anxiety. We had to learn to read his fears and back off, not counting on our calendar when a child should attain certain skills in life.

Sixth grade came, and instead of one teacher, now there were seven teachers to try to understand and help our son. Oh, if his teachers only knew how hard this was for him they might take the time to find out how to help! "Jason can do such great things in math. He just struggles so hard to stay on task," the teacher explained to me. "How do we help him stay on task?" asked the teacher. I thought, "This is not my question to answer. Why doesn't the teacher know? Surely there have been other ADD children in the teacher's classroom."

Jason had other problems that surfaced since he became eleven that alienated him from the other children. He didn't know how to communicate effectively in the social world of school. This made him more depressed. The cafeteria was loaded with peers, and yet, Jason chose to sit alone. Then, there was the playground, before school, during lunch, and after school. Jason did not know what to do as the boys continually bullied him. He was afraid to be touched, and they threatened and tormented him. Jason told me he chose to act crazy to get them off his back, and it worked.

He was also obsessed with getting his work done in class. He was disappointed when he couldn't be like everyone else. Despite his peers, the teachers loved him. He modeled what every teacher wanted. He never broke the rules. He lived by them. He tried hard, wanted to learn, hated to fail. Yet no matter how good he acted, he had many days when he was unable to motivate himself. "Teachers, can you help us, walk beside us, work with us, to help our son? Let's learn together, so Jason can get better."

In the spring semester of sixth grade, he began to feel like a failure. His grades began to drop. I found out that he was having trouble keeping up with his books in his locker during school. Jason chose to carry his books around all day at school. I purchased a set of books, so he could have a set at home and not have any more trouble remembering the books that were needed for homework.

At the age of eleven, we sought a psychiatrist's opinion. The doctor was sure Jason was suffering from depression, so he prescribed an anti-depressant. Within a week's time, Jason became lethargic at school and began to talk to himself more. I called the doctor, and he prescribed an EEG. The school staff was already calling me at home, because Jason was walking around lethargic and sluggish. I quickly took him from school to the hospital. As he lay quietly, they began to test him. About five minutes into the test, he began to have reactions that looked like seizures. I was asked by the technician if this had happened before, and I told the technician, "No, and I am not leaving this hospital until you can tell me what is wrong with our son!" Since Jason continued to have the seizures, he was taken to a short-term behavioral psychiatric hospital located directly next door to the main hospital. In this one day, our lives began to change forever.

As they transported us to the hospital, he continued having the seizures. People were starring at us. I was bewildered by what was happening to our son. For the first time in my life, I felt out of control emotionally. I was in a state of panic. I felt very weak and was trying to hold back the tears. I felt a great need for John to hold me to tell me everything was going to be alright, but I was alone and afraid.

6

The Picture Revealed

The day that the mystery ended and our puzzle finally had a picture was when the psychiatrist diagnosed Jason. He stated, "Your son, Jason, has Asperger's Syndrome (AS), a form of autism, which includes depression, Obsessive Compulsive Disorder (OCD), and Attention Deficit Disorder (ADD) with a written language disability." After two weeks in the hospital, eleven years of waiting and searching for answers came to an end. We could finally put a name to all the frustrations, fears and behavioral problems.

We then looked to the doctor for answers. I asked patiently, "Now that we know what is wrong how do we fix all this?" "You can't," he said. "We can treat only the symptoms that seem to cause Jason trouble in living a productive life." I thought to myself as my mind wandered over all that had been said, "What constitutes a productive life?" Now that a name could be placed on Jason's behavioral problems, I wanted to fix it all. John's response was a little different from mine. He knew Jason was different at a young age, but the problem did not hit home for him until Jason was diagnosed. Every parent wants their child to have a perfect life without suffering. This situation was very hard for both of us to accept.

We were both shocked and relieved that we finally knew what was wrong. We wrestled with whether to tell Jason and others about the situation. We decided to be open about it, so he could learn to work with his disability and know why he was in the hospital a month. We felt he had a right to know, especially at the age of twelve. We knew that the diagnosis would help him calm some of his anxieties. Yet, new ones would surface.

There never was a right, perfect way to tell Jason that something was wrong with him. We wanted to encourage him. We desired to share the truth that we all face obstacles in life, but we must learn how to overcome them. He had many obstacles to overcome. I wondered where to begin. He remained in the hospital for a month. That provided me with time to learn about Asperger's Syndrome, ADD, depression and OCD. I searched for definitions that could help me understand more about what each diagnosis meant. I learned that Asperger's "is a lifelong social disorder characterized by a lack of empathy, little ability to form relationships, one-sided conversations, clumsy movements, and intense absorption in special interests."[4] Obsessive Compulsive Disorder was defined as "obsessional mental activity which leads to compulsive behavior. Obsession-an idea or thought lodges in the mind that cannot be forgotten. Compulsion-unreasonable need to behave in a certain way."[5] John and I were trying to learn how to accept it all, so we could teach Jason to accept it.

All of my life I had thought autism meant the person could not speak, banged his head against the walls, and would not look at people. I believed that all autistic people seemed to be in their own little world where others could not reach them. Then I saw the movie "Rain Man." Jason was young, but I saw traits in Raymond, the character Dustin Hoffman played, that Jason portrayed on a daily basis. I saw similar rituals and compared the structured environment that was critical to Raymond's well being to the structured environment we had created for Jason. This I saw in our son, but I believed that Jason could not be autistic because he talked and had a high IQ, I thought, "Then again, he does bang his hand against his head when he is agitated, and he flaps his hands when he is stressed." He was like that autistic puzzle we so often see. Some pieces fit, others don't. Later, I discovered that Jason had Asperger's Syndrome, which has some symptoms similar to autism and some that are different from autism. We had to continue to pray for the pieces to fit together, so we could see Jason clearly and understand him. We had a strong belief and trust in God. We believed that He was in control of our lives. We were comforted knowing Jason had a strong faith as well.

One sunny Sunday morning when Jason was only four years old, John and Jason went to church. As they were traveling, Jason asked his father, "What is sin?" After John replied, Jason questioned, "Can I ask Jesus to come into my heart?" He prayed with John and accepted Christ as his Savior. He had such a precious faith. As he grew older, we often found him on his knees in his bedroom praying. At one time, it was as early as 5 a.m. before school that he chose to take time to pray.

His spiritual passion was so deep that one Sunday he came to us and told us he couldn't go to church until we called Tim and got him to accept Christ. Tim was a neighbor boy whom Jason only knew slightly. He played with Luke and seldom went to church. Jason was convinced that we had to speak to Tim immediately. We compromised with Jason after 30 minutes of a long, confusing, frustrating conversation. We decided that he would call Tim and ask him to go to church. That was fine with Jason, so we helped him to call Tim on the phone. He couldn't come, but Jason was determined to get him saved. One Sunday morning after church service, I found him praying in the sanctuary all alone. Afterwards, I asked him why. He said, "Because Susan needs prayer. She has leprosy." When I investigated the circumstances, I found that Susan was a friend both at school and church who had chicken pox all over her face. Jason just assumed she had leprosy.

Jason saw the Bible as black or white. There was no gray. When he listened to a sermon or read the Bible on his own, he often struggled to understand what "grace" or "humble" meant. What may seem clear to one man may not be clear to another. He believed that "humble" meant turning the other cheek. When a boy hit him at school, he just turned the other cheek and said something like, "Go ahead and hit this one too." We knew we had to be careful with what we said or did around Jason because he took things literally. He knew his Bible too, so it was hard to sneak one over on him. I am so proud today that Jason and Luke have a strong faith in God. That gives me great comfort.

7

Finding a Home

Jason came home in March on an outpatient basis, so he could continue to get help with his school work at the hospital during the day. He continued to act sluggish and would not participate in conversation. His medications were not helping. The doctors changed his medications.

One afternoon, I came to the hospital early because he had an orthodontist appointment. While driving to the doctor's office, Jason asked if he could go to a dance that they were having at his junior high school on Friday night. It was a Wednesday, and I was already having a hard week, because the staff at the hospital informed me that he was not cooperating during the school hours and not participating appropriately with group discussions. My decision was to tell him that he could go on Friday to the dance if, and only if, the hospital staff saw some improvement in his behavior.

Jason became extremely angry as if I had told him, "No." At this time he was twelve years old and quite strong. He then began to say he wanted to kill himself and me. He began to hit me as I drove down the interstate. I put up my right arm to defend myself, as he continually hit me over and over again until I thought my arm was broken. I began to cry. I felt that my best option was to keep driving, and get to the orthodontist as quickly as possible to get help.

I favored my right arm, and when Jason began to see me crying he let up. I was able to get to the office. He came in behind me, sat down, and immediately went to sleep. I called John for help. He came to get us to drive us back to the hospital. The hospital readmitted him for his suicidal and homicidal tendencies. I have never seen Jason like that again. I believed that a specific medication caused him to become that way. Within the next few days, doctors concluded that he needed a long-term care facility. His life was taking a turn we never expected. Our son was hurting, and I could not fix him. I had to let go of him, and let someone else care for him, so he could begin to live in this world again. I had to turn to the only One who could really help us, God.

John and I did not know where to begin. The hospital provided us with the name of an educational consultant who could help us in our search for long-term care facilities. For a $500 fee the consultant agreed to research and provide us with four to six facilities that would be appropriate for Jason. She also provided psychological testing in order for us to have accurate records of his educational and medical needs.

As the consultant began her job, I became busy looking on the Internet and library for any leads. The need was for a long-term hospital, preferably homey, small, close to home in South Carolina for non-violent children. Jason was far from violent, aside from his episode in the car. A psychiatrist tested him and concluded that he was a bright, intellectual-oriented boy, with an IQ ranging from 109–122, depending on his state of depression. Within two weeks, the consultant had concluded research for a facility. We were left with the awesome task of visiting the facilities that were recommended. For Jason's benefit, we felt that we had to decide as quickly as possible.

Meanwhile, he remained in the hospital until we could transition him to a long-term care facility. The consultant's first and foremost selection was a facility in Evergreen, Colorado, called Forest Heights Lodge. There were no suitable institutions in our state. We agreed with her choice, based on what we read about the Lodge. We all went for a visit to Evergreen to see what Jason's reaction was. Colorado was so far away, however, I knew I wanted the most appropriate place, so distance was not considered to be a factor.

We spent two days just getting to know the area. Forest Heights Lodge is situated in the Rocky Mountains of Colorado. A large cabin-like building had enough room to house 24 boys, a school, and a kitchen with a large great room. The hospital staff seemed very professional and caring. They seemed to put his needs first. After we visited the Lodge, Jason asked the staff if he could come live there.

The next step was for June, the social worker, to come visit in our home for three days to observe how he lived. When she arrived, she spent her time assisting me with filling out all the necessary papers and observing Jason in our home. She wrote down all his idiosyncrasies, like the type of clothing he wore. She took note of his favorite foods, the things he was allergic to, and his favorite activities. John and I were pleased with how thorough the staff was in making sure they knew Jason's needs and wants. We were all set to go.

My job was to raise money for his care at the Lodge at $5,000 a month. As time grew near for him to leave, my heart began to feel relieved that he had somewhere to go to help him, yet I grieved about him leaving. Letting him go was the hardest thing I have ever had to do. Jason was twelve years old, so young, so vulnerable. He took going to the Lodge in stride, probably because anywhere was better than remaining in a psychiatric hospital after almost four months.

I kept myself busy trying to meet Jason's needs and arranging medical records that were useful for the Lodge and for the school district. I was frantically trying to come up with a plan to get the funds for Forest Heights Lodge. Meanwhile, the school district was contacted to begin meetings to determine if they would pay for his schooling in Colorado.

My responsibility was to prove that the school district was not able to sufficiently meet his educational needs. Therefore, they would pay his individual allotment of $600 a month to the hospital for as long as Jason remained in Colorado. I also needed for support our psychiatrist, a psychologist, and the lawyer from Protection and Advocacy (P&A). Every state is required by law to provide assistance for the legal rights of children within the school district. In our state, P&A fulfilled this role. All these professionals were needed to meet with the school district's psychiatrist, psychologist, social worker, specific teachers, and Jason's middle school principal. This meeting is part of the Individualized Education Plan (IEP).

I soon discovered that Jason could qualify for Social Security Income (SSI) as long as he remained in a long-term care facility, which meant getting records from birth to present. SSI allocates an allotment of money that the federal government provides monthly to those who are considered to be disabled. I quickly sent for the medical and educational records, and found myself ready to go to the SSI office. As I sat down with the representative, she was so thrilled that I had all of his medical records ready for copies to be made. She diligently searched for the title number under which Jason would qualify. I was amazed when she informed me that he would receive $550 a month while he lived in a long-term care facility. SSI would take approximately three months to process. However, with medical records in hand, it could be sooner. I once again was amazed to get an SSI check beginning in July when he was to be admitted to the Lodge.

Meanwhile, I continually worked on preparing for the school district's IEP meeting. I expected real problems convincing the district to pay for his schooling, but I knew I had a lot of professional help to assist me. We met for three hours to determine what his educational needs were. During those three hours, I struggled to consistently show them that Jason's needs were far above what they could provide.

His ongoing depression and new diagnosis of Asperger's Syndrome, Obsessive Compulsive Disorder, Attention Deficit Disorder, and written language disability, demanded one-on-one direction, and when ready, a small classroom setting to teach him organization and study skills. Teachers came to share their insights, but I felt so angry inside when his principal stated, "I don't know what the problem is here, the child made good grades." I sat across the table holding my tongue and thinking, "What is the importance of grades if his grades are dropping quickly, he is struggling from lack of organization and is depressed?" The principal barely knew Jason, and yet, he made such rash statements!

At the end of the session, it was uncertain whether he would qualify for an alternative educational placement. As we began to leave, the social worker approached us and stated that, although the school district staff felt they could adequately meet Jason's needs, they were willing to pay $600 a month beginning that August and continuing through May. The school system chose to do what was best for Jason, and I was truly thankful for the time and effort that they put into his IEP.

Therefore, I had worked hard to successfully raise $600 from the school district, and $550 from SSI, leaving only $3,850 left to raise per month. I strongly believed that the money would be there when the time came for payment. We knew we had to rely on our families to help us get through the year. I believe that when God wants us to do something, He always provides the means. All of Luke's surgeries were paid for by insurance, us, and friends. The past for me was a barometer showing us what God can and will do, and we believed that. I was elated with joy! Jason's financial needs were being met, but deep down I knew that the time was nearing for me to physically and emotionally let my son go.

8

Forest Heights Lodge

He remained in the hospital until the day we were to travel to Colorado. Jason and I flew to Denver while Luke and John drove to Colorado with the rest of Jason's belongings. The doctor put him on a medicine to help keep his anxiety down while traveling and to help him deal with all the changes. So many changes occurred so fast that I was numb from exhaustion. Yet, I was at peace knowing that the Lodge was right for Jason and us. To begin at the Lodge we had to deposit $5,000 up front. The expenses to travel ranged from $300 to $500 each time we came to visit depending on the air fare. I remember being amazed that whenever we needed money, it was there. I believed God wanted him in Colorado because He provided the finances.

Jason did well traveling to Evergreen, but I was so concerned that he would change his mind, and the staff at the Lodge would not convince him to stay. John and I checked him in. Jason was accepted at Forest Heights Lodge with open arms by warm, friendly people, in a caring atmosphere. John and I helped him unpack his belongings, and the time to leave came quickly. My heart became heavy as I said good-bye to my older son. I never felt so much loss in one day, and yet, I was reminded once again that this was what was best for him. My husband, John, and our younger son, Luke, age ten, needed me too! I cried uncontrollably as we drove away. I wanted to allow my feelings to overwhelm me, to be depressed over my son leaving home at the age of twelve. But, I know I needed a strong faith, a good perspective and trust that God was in control of all of our lives. I had faith that God, and only God could get me through this time in my life. The separation of a child from his mother can be devastating. But I chose not to let it be. My life would never be the same, but I had to go on. I had to let go of Jason.

The Lodge's staff directed us not to contact Jason for at least 4 to 6 weeks to allow him to adjust to his new environment. I continued to appropriate our money for the hospital as daily life in our family returned to normal, as normal as could be, knowing that Jason was getting the best of care. We trusted God that time and distance could not separate the love we had for each other. One evening as I lay awake thinking of Jason many miles away from home, I wrote this poem:

A CHILD MILES FROM HOME, NEAR IN THE HEART

Life without Jason is hard I know,
Three plates at the table not four in a row.
Each day I miss watching him by inches grow,
Each precious moment I do not know
For in Colorado, he skis in the snow.

Where is he? Or what he says there are others each day to hear.
The times on the phone once a week are held by us so dear.
Maybe we will see him ten times a year,
But no one knows what it can be to rear,
Jason, our son, 13 who lives so far and yet in my heart so near.

The promises of God keep a hedge of protection
around him each day.
The Holy Spirit knows how much I love and pray,
That one day he will come home to us and stay.

I will remember one thing the rest of Jason's life on earth,
He is not mine, but God's, a gift from birth!

Count each moment as precious with your child,
Because God can call him away for awhile.
It is then you should be able to stand and say with a smile,
"He is not mine but God's each and every mile!"

They grow and one day you give them a quarter to phone,
But only God can guide them wherever they roam from home.

So look up and smile today and pray,
"Thank you, God our child is here with us today,
Given by you to show them the way."

If I look above the reality,
The Spirit of God will reveal to me,
The table does not just have plates for three.
The fourth is there as by faith I see,
My son, Jason, here, near, and dear to me.

Many nights passed by and often I needed to remind myself that God was holding him in His hands.

The staff at the Lodge chose treatment for the children using the "attachment model." The attachment model basically teaches a child to trust his environment and interpersonal relationships once again. Jason, for some reason, never trusted anyone other than John, me, Joyce, and a few close family relatives. Jason's anxiety and frustrations kept him from trusting others and his environment. The staff at the Lodge helped him to trust his environment and others again. Jason also focused on sensory integration techniques within the framework of his treatment plan. Bicycles and rollerblading were encouraged to increase coordination and balance. This program was developed because "children and adults with autism may have a dysfunctional sensory system. Sometimes one or more senses are either over-or under-reactive to stimulation."[6]

Jason is sensitive to smells and touch, which includes the clothes that he wears. Smells are a serious problem with him. Many times we were surprised by anxiety that prevailed no matter where he was. He struggled with car exhaust. Although he could not avoid it, he wanted to get away from it as fast as he could. He had adapted to some odors, but most created Obsessive Compulsive type behaviors. Mildew is a common odor that he has never been able to overcome. He will not go places that have a strong smell. We've never been able to talk him out of the sensitivity problems, nor has he changed. This has been a lifelong struggle, and we have just had to work through each incident. Many Asperger's Syndrome children have sensory problems either with smell, touch, hearing, or over stimulation. That is why Jason does not like to be touched.

He also struggles with the discomfort of clothing he wears. From the age of caring about what he wore, he has always had to have labels removed from his shirts. Going shopping was a very tiresome chore. Jason would not wear any jeans or fabric that was denim. He did not look at whether it was 50% cotton, or polyester, or 100% cotton. He felt the fabric with his fingers, and if it passed the test of comfort, he wanted to buy it. We could spend all day searching for the right, just right, clothing. Shopping became easier after years of experience because I learned exactly what he had to have.

The pants that were like Dockers would do just fine. Since Jason was eight he has been wearing this type of pants. Shorts were "a must" to be worn under all pants. Usually, he preferred the plain old cotton T-shirts. He likes the colors black, blue and red. Since Jason was fourteen, he began wearing a hooded sweat shirt at all times. He preferred zipper sweatshirts. He wore his sweatshirt whether we were in a restaurant, or he was outside in the heat. Jason tolerated the cold nights or days with his simple sweatshirt and a light jacket. He did not complain about whether it was hot or too cold as long as he was comfortable. He said he wore clothes the way he did because, "It is predictable, and that is the way I like things."

His lack of awareness to temperature baffled me. He once sat in the car at his brother's soccer game, refusing to watch the game. He sat with a sweatshirt on in 85 degree weather in a closed car with the windows up, sweating, and content to remain so. I could only be guided by his reactions or behaviors, not by what was proper for the situation. If everyone was wearing the same thing, Jason would definitely do the opposite. He did not appear to want to belong with his peers or to be accepted by them. He had his own idiosyncrasies, and that was Jason. Life was too short to question why, or to try to make him change. He would change only when he was ready.

Learning to tie shoes was a challenging task, so he preferred the Velcro type. Thank God for Velcro! So much time and energy were saved by having Velcro on my son's feet! Now that he is in his twenties, Jason wears his tennis shoes all the time one size larger than his size, so he can slip them on. He just does not like to have to tie on shoes.

Jason did not respond to pain like we do. When he was placed in the hospital at two years old for dehydration, he was put on an I.V. He just sat there and watched the doctors put the needle in his arm. When they took his blood, he just stared at the blood, and did not even whimper. I thought that to be quite unusual.

Sports such as baseball and basketball were played at the Lodge to help the young people learn social skills with peers. Camping and hiking trips through the Rockies helped him learn to work with others. Winter skiing quickly became his favorite sport. He loved cross-country skiing through the beautiful mountains in Colorado.

School began when Jason chose to go to school. Jason had one-on-one instruction for three months. Then, he was moved to a small classroom. He did well in this atmosphere. As the depression slowly lifted his school work showed signs of improvement. They gave him structured homework time at the Lodge. Somehow they were able to get him to do his homework. They worked on his organizational skills and tried to get him to focus better on his work. Jason continued to work slowly, but he kept up with the pace of the small classroom.

The staff concentrated on Jason's depression first, and then worked with him with regard to his Asperger's Syndrome. Everything had a purpose for teaching the boys about life and their environment. Social skills were important when living with 24 boys. Jason was learning independent living skills as the staff taught him to cook, wash his own clothes, and be responsible for his room. The Lodge was truly a family environment that taught Jason about his feelings, how to acknowledge them, and accept them on a daily basis.

9

Healing Amidst the Pain

Jason was doing well, but now my life had to adjust to another turn in the road. One September afternoon, my mother called and informed me she had cancer in her chest cavity. The doctors believed strongly that she had a good chance to beat it with chemotherapy. I was devastated and began to feel that there was a possibility she could die. As the weeks went by, mom's initial diagnosis changed. The doctors found a tumor on her spine. I was told to get a check-up immediately, and to continue check-ups each year thereafter.

When I went to my doctor for the mammogram, my heart felt heavy with the question of how long mom had to live. As I waited for the doctor, the nurse put me in a room with a video tape on cancer and its stages of development. I tried to hide the tears as the tape described the stage five cancer my mother had. "Stage five! How long would she live? What are the chances of survival?" I thought. The nurse came in, and I told her what was upsetting me. She asked me to stay to talk to the doctor about my questions. In a few minutes she took me into the doctor's office where he gently asked me questions regarding my mother's diagnosis. He began to share that although he had not seen my mother, he was fairly sure she had only six weeks to two months to live. My mother was going to die, and I could not do anything except pray for God's timing.

On September 29th, 1990 my father called me to tell me my mom had died. My mom awoke from a restless night in pain, so dad prepared to take her to the hospital. While she was dressing, she fell down and died from a blood clot, which may have been caused by the chemotherapy treatment.

Jason flew to New Orleans, Louisiana, where we picked him up and took him to Hammond, Louisiana, for the memorial. The memorial service was comforting. The only comment Jason had occurred during the memorial service when he stated, "Being dead is not all that bad, Mom." I didn't have a response to that statement; I just thought, "Jason is Jason."

There were times when he spoke words that were cruel or seemed intentionally rude. When he was anxious or tired he became echolalic. Then, there were times when he spoke uncanny words of wisdom. One time he came home from West Virginia where he was visiting our friend Joyce. She stayed with us a few days. As she began to leave and her car was backing out of the driveway, Jason ran into the yard crying, "She's taking my heart! She's taking my heart!" I cried too, knowing what he meant and how his words expressed his pain and loss. He could, at times, speak words full of meaning. But usually, he struggled to express his feelings. He also encouraged people with his words. Once when we visited a church for the first time, Jason was about ten years old. As we all greeted each other throughout the congregation, he often greeted everyone with a handshake and a, "Hi." He tried to shake as many hands as he could. He found a blind lady in one of the front pews. Her name was Sheila. He walked up to Sheila and whispered in her ear, "Isn't it great that all you see is God?" Sheila was so touched by his words.

Christmastime came quickly. Jason was flown home free by Delta Airlines as a Christmas gift to us. Our family was once again together, and I was so happy to have a loving, caring home to watch Jason and Luke grow into manhood. Teenage years were ahead, and

I felt that it was so important to remember what my mom always portrayed in her life, unconditional love. All seven of her children were accepted just the way they were. I believed that I must not only remember how important unconditional love is, but live it. Jason and Luke would need all the love and acceptance I could give them. He was doing very well at the Lodge. We were thankful that in three short months he had adjusted to the structure and environment of the Lodge. Changes were not easy for him. It often took him much more time to adapt to anywhere we went, especially to a change in where he was living. He normally was a lot more anxious than usual during the time of adjustment then he appeared to be this time.

The staff of the Lodge chose to meet with us in February for a therapy session. John and I were able to meet the financial costs of September, October, and November when we combined all the SSI and School District monies together with our savings. Our insurance company began to pay for February, March, and April. Therapy sessions were basically a time to go over his progress, to meet with staff and teachers, and to give input on what could be done for him to improve at the Lodge. Suggestions were made regarding how to structure our home to assist Jason in reducing his anxiety and frustration levels. Each visit ended with a special time to take Jason from the Lodge to spend quality time together. We often got a hotel room and stayed a night or two with him. As visits continued, he knew a lot about the Denver area and took us to his favorite places. One or both of us tried so hard to visit Jason at least every six weeks.

One of the biggest changes I noticed was that Jason began to tell me he loved me more often. Since the age of eight, he would not allow anyone to touch him. At the Lodge he gave me hugs when I came to see him. Jason continued giving me hugs as he grew older. He started reaching out to others in his own timing, but he continues to struggle with others touching him to this day.

When a year had gone by, he still needed treatment in a long-term care facility. The insurance company agreed to continue to pay every three months if we continued to pay. John and I made it through the first year, so we knew we could make it one more. John's parents, my father, and my great aunt sent $5,000 to the Lodge to help with his medical care. My great uncle died in November 1991, and we were surprised when we inherited $20,000!

Although, our needs were being met financially, and Jason and Luke were doing well, I wasn't. I began to go into a deep depression. The doctors put me in a short-term psychiatric hospital to observe how medication I was taking for my bipolar disorder affected me. They changed my medicines and provided me with two new anti-depressants. I just did not handle stress well. One of the problems was all the stress that I felt in dealing with Jason's situation. I felt anxious all the time. In addition to that, finding the funds to meet our needs and our sons' needs monthly finally got the best of me. John and I decided it would be best to let John take over the financial burden. Although I still worried, John took on the bills. I knew I had to let Jason go, but inside, as a mother, I wanted my son home. I knew that I could not take care of him at that time, and I wasn't sure I could in the future. The stress was too much for me. I remembered Job in the Bible, who lost everything but gained a deeper relationship with God. I needed that deeper relationship with God to make it. It took months for the adjustments in medication to work and for me to slowly heal.

The money was always there, even when the insurance called to say they were terminating Jason's care in April of 1992. We were able to pay until July 15th when he was to come home. What a miracle! Amidst all the pain we were able to financially pay for two years at the Lodge, so he could have the best of care. Jason made steady progress at Forest Heights over the two year time period. No medications were suggested, and his anxiety and frustration levels were down considerably. The hospital provided so much structure and life skills that Jason's confidence grew tremendously. He seemed so calm. The biggest change was less depression with no medication because of the highly structured environment. He learned to socialize better and express his feelings.

The Lodge engaged Jason in snow skiing, bicycling, hiking, roller blading, basketball, baseball, and football, which built his confidence and strengthened his coordination. He enjoyed the outdoors now and found he could acquire the skills for a sport at his own pace and succeed. He learned to live and cope with various kinds of boys. He took responsibility for his own problems and completed chores around the Lodge. Jason still struggled with his Obsessive Compulsive tendencies. He believed in extreme cleanliness to the point of making a cleaning job immaculate. Jason took extremely long showers just talking to himself and laughing. When asked to sweep the sidewalk he felt the necessity of cleaning the cracks as well.

Of course, in the winter time, Evergreen was covered with snow, which meant skiing was in order for recreation time with Jason. I could not ski because of my back condition, but by the time we visited, Jason had already begun to master cross-country skiing.

Jason went on a camping trip in Colorado. The hospital had an annual camping trip when they hiked and camped on a 14,000 foot mountain. He went for a week. When he returned, I called to inquire how his trip went. "It went great Mom, but I forgot my socks, so I only had one pair the whole week." I asked, "What did you do to stay clean?" "Killing the bacteria was easy," he exclaimed. "I just took a shower each night, and took my socks off, and filled my socks up with soap from the soap dispenser in the shower stall. Once I dried off, and dressed, I put the socks back on with my shoes which killed the bacteria in my feet for the whole week!" Jason truly believed that this would kill the bacteria, and his solution worked. I found it amazing how hard he worked in order to solve his problems.

His progress in school was remarkable. He completed eighth grade and had learned how to better organize his time to finish homework. When Jason was asked what he learned at the Lodge and the impact it had on his life, he replied, "The Lodge taught me that I do not have to have my parents. I can live without them. At the Lodge, I began to think for myself and whether God existed. I learned God was real. I got used to Colorado and all that structure." The challenge was yet to come as Jason neared the time of his transfer back to home in Aiken, South Carolina. The Lodge staff agreed that they would put him on lithium when he was discharged. This was to help with his depressive episodes. Coping outside of the Lodge would be a big transition for him, especially when it came to his schooling. I was so used to having Jason cared for that my heart filled with doubts. I asked myself, "How I can provide a good, loving, structured atmosphere for our son? Can I put the past aside and reach out to a new future with Jason?"

10

Coming Home

I could hardly believe it. After two long years, Jason was coming home! I quickly contacted the public schools, so I could have an IEP meeting in May, before the schools closed for the summer. I also contacted a private school in Aiken as another option for Jason's education. Aiken's private school provided me with an interview while the public school system arranged an IEP meeting in late May. Forest Heights Lodge's last responsibility was to make sure we had a school for Jason to attend in the fall. June, the social worker for Jason at the Lodge, flew down in May to meet with the pubic schools to make sure that his IEP was in order and his transition went smoothly.

I visited several middle schools, met with their principals and special education teachers. Jason did not feel ready for high school, so the decision was made for him to repeat eighth grade. He had an above average IQ, but his special needs would be best met in the environment of a special education classroom. As he progressed, the goal was to gradually allow him to mainstream into the science and math classrooms. Math and science were his strong subjects and the ones in which he had the most confidence. I was able to meet with Aiken's private school administration once Jason returned home. They wanted to meet with him personally. We toured the building and grounds. We found the school small and very structured. They even had tutors if he needed them. Upon looking at his application and consulting with others, they felt that they could not adequately meet Jason's educational needs. It was a nice way to say they did not want to even try to educate my son. They decided that his disabilities warranted greater attention than they could provide. I wish they had known how much my son needed a small, structured environment to meet his educational needs. The county public schools became our only option.

Jason needed special attention in public school. He had problems with concentration. His lack of social skills continued to be a factor that needed to be addressed. He also needed his stress level monitored in school. Jason struggled with a written language disability which affected his English assignments. Verbal testing was needed. In our state after a child reaches the age of fourteen it is mandated that he receive Vocational Rehabilitation Services. Since Jason had an above average IQ and had made the honor roll in his college-prep classes, the IEP team decided that he would most likely attend college. Therefore, his Vocational Rehabilitation focused on preparing him for college.

All the decisions were made for his education within the special education department by his IEP. The Lodge had made a list of requirements for the schools: 1) structured setting with clear expectations, 2) low student/teacher ratio, 3) environment where staff are comfortable recognizing differences and meeting those differences, 4) opportunity to participate in scheduled non-academic activities after school hours. I included within the IEP, preferential seating close to the teacher, same seating every day, and select teachers who had a disciplined and structured atmosphere within their classrooms. Jason was ready to come home, and both our family and his school were ready for him.

Two years had gone by, and he had grown a lot. Once again, change would not be easy. Jason came home in July. John and I tried to limit our expectations and aim for taking one step at a time.

In August our extended family went on our annual trip to the beach, and by then, he was comfortably back at home and adjusting quite well.

We structured his room to better meet his needs, so everything was in order at home. We chose to continue the check mark system in which we made a list of chores, and he checked them off daily as he completed them. In turn, we provided him with an allowance. He would save ten percent in his savings account, tithe ten percent to the church, and spend the rest. This helped Jason to learn consistently how to manage his money.

We worked hard to teach Jason living skills within our family, so he would learn to become independent. Each task he was given had to be given step-by-step with one direction at a time. We often stopped what we were doing and showed him how to complete the task. He worked so slowly, and unfortunately, the Lodge could not change that. Completing the work was what was important to us no matter how long it took. Given Jason's type of disability, we could not easily discern what was helping him. We found this to be perplexing and sometimes discouraging.

Summers always seemed to go by so quickly. Jason's younger brother was going to Jackson Middle while Jason attended Temple Middle. The Temple Middle School staff made a concerted effort to insure Jason would have a smooth transition. As he began eighth grade, we continuously watched him to make sure that his life had a minimal amount of stress in it.

He began his day in the self-contained classroom where he organized his books and completed any remaining homework assignments. English and history were taught in that classroom. Jason was mainstreamed in math, science and music. The Lodge staff had found that he had a keen interest in music, therefore, they encouraged him to join band. He returned to his self-contained class for lunch and at the end of the day for a study hour to prepare his homework assignments and organize his books for the next day.

Homework was still a burden. However, Jason's organizational skills were better, and he was able to distinctly tell someone when he was angry, anxious, or frustrated. Feelings were always hard to express, but Jason had overcome some of its barriers. His coping skills were so much better, but he continued to respond incorrectly when someone physically hurt him. Jason's classroom was supposed to protect him from the mainstream problems, especially the violence. Most of the kids were non-violent like Jason, but there are always a few kids who don't follow the rules.

I was so thankful that the hard work of setting up his IEP was paying off, and Jason was adjusting well to Temple Middle School. We felt blessed that the two years in Colorado were a turning point for Jason. We were able to successfully transition Jason back home. The future looked bright with Jason being home, adjusting to school, and coping well with his depression.

II

Labeling Jason

I was happy and relaxed during the 1992–93 school year and, except for the homework, stress was minimal. Jason adjusted well at school and also at home. When we went out to dinner, he made decisions quicker, so ordering our food was not a big issue any longer. We still gave him extra time with the menu, but he was able to make a decision in a reasonable amount of time. In the past, making a decision was a great obstacle for Jason. Forest Heights Lodge did a superb job with him. I was so thankful.

Choosing a high school was not an easy task. Jason would now be interacting with seven teachers during the day. He still did not like the thought of having a locker, so we needed to establish a resource room where he could store his books. Since he did so well at Temple Junior High School we felt he may be ready for what Jefferson High School had to offer.

Although Jason was mainstreamed, his homeroom and resource teacher were the same. He used his resource room to organize his books and keep up with homework assignments. Teachers were selected for math, English, German, band, history and science. I purchased two sets of books, so we would always have one set at the house for homework purposes. According to his IEP, the teachers were required to provide discipline and a highly structured environment. They had to be willing to use alternative teaching methods to meet his needs. Creativity was important, because if the teacher wasn't creative, Jason became bored.

He took the special education bus to school because the kids on the regular bus called him all kinds of mean names. I don't know why kids have to be so cruel. It seems like they have to pick on someone, and it is usually the underdog. I don't know how this affected Jason, because he just let them be cruel. It hurt me to know others were taking advantage of our son. What concerned me was that Jason chose to live in his "intellectual world." I tried to get him to live in "our world." How could I ever succeed as long as children were so cruel, which forced him to withdraw into himself?

Jason was sixteen and in ninth grade, yet, he had no interest in learning how to drive. He had adjusted to all of his classes, and the teachers liked him a lot. They all seemed to be a good fit for him. His math teacher liked the theories that he brought to class. Jason did not want to just do the math problems. He wanted to know the theories behind them.

Three weeks passed since school began, and he was doing well with all the changing circumstances and so many teachers. He loved his German class. I took him to school some days and watched as he went into class. If he got there early, he waited in the library. I began to notice that he was not going into the building, but was waiting at the front door. As students went in, he opened the door for them and said, "Hi." Well, this kept on until the tardy bell rang for class. Then, he quickly went inside and got to class on time.

I checked into the situation and found out that he not only opened the door for everyone at the beginning of the day, but also, on the way to the cafeteria and at the end of the day. When he got to the doors to go into the cafeteria, he stopped and let everyone else go first, sometimes missing his lunch. I brought this to the attention of the resource room teacher, and he saw to it that Jason had time for lunch. Jason told me he opened all the doors for everyone because he wanted to start a revival. He wanted everyone to join in and go to the flag pole each Wednesday to pray before school. I thought he had a big heart for God. I did not want to discourage him.

Jason chose to be in the marching band in ninth grade. Since we knew he couldn't march on the field, the band director chose to place him on the percussion team which remained stationary, off the field. John and I were excited to see him do so well in band and travel with the band. The band director chose someone to buddy with Jason while they were traveling. That way, he would not get lost and would be at the bus on time.

Once again, except for homework, ninth grade at the high school was transitionally successful from the middle school. He did get lost on occasion, and we had to search the high school for him. Always, we found him in a teacher's room discussing his homework, or as he called it, "picking their brains." He just went off on a tangent and did not look at his watch to see where he was supposed to be.

I was deeply concerned about him being labeled in high school. If the students did not know of his disability, they would not patronize him. Labels were important for the teachers so that his educational needs could be met. Labels helped professionals to obtain the right medications for him and understand what his struggles were. For John and me, they were helpful in gaining insight into Jason's behavior and meeting his daily needs. The more specific the diagnostic label, the better informed the professionals would be in meeting Jason's needs. Labels had their place, but we had to be careful.

I do not care for labels, but I know now that if you don't have them, it is hard to get the correct services. Also, labels help parents to put their child's needs in perspective. How long I searched for the knowledge of how to relate to Jason! With a diagnosis, it became easier to understand some of his behaviors. The diagnosis enabled me to access information to help me work with him. It also provided me with a way to help others understand him and his needs. As John and I read Tony Atwood's book, *Asperger's Syndrome*, we were able to come to understand Jason's multiple disorders realistically.

Labels are used to assist. Yet, for Jason every label had to be taken out of his shirts. He ripped them out if necessary. They had to go! The labels bothered him like a gnat on his neck. If peace of mind for him meant taking out every label, no matter how time consuming or trivial it seemed to me, then so be it. However, I used medical labels to help others to understand Jason's special needs. He had distinct and unique needs that had to be addressed properly, or his needs would go unmet.

So, labels do have a purpose for the proper treatment of some special needs children. I often asked myself the question, "When are labels not useful?" Irritating labels in Jason's shirts were not useful. The other kind of labels that are a hindrance are those that keep our children in a cage. Labels should not determine who children are, or who they will become. They should just determine how to help them reach their goals. So, I will use whatever diagnostic label that will be the most helpful in order to get Jason one more step closer to an independent life. Jason said, "I don't want to be in this world. I like my intellectual one." I pray for him to want both worlds so he can make a difference in this world no matter how small or great. I believe God made him for a reason. Labels don't cure, but they do reduce the confusion in the world of autism.

12

No Friends

When the teachers and I developed his tenth grade IEP, I found that we had been blessed again with teachers who were organized and enforced discipline in their classrooms. His English, band, and resource teachers were the same as in ninth grade. Jason had very little adjusting to do, since the faculty and staff were now used to him and his idiosyncrasies. He continued to open the doors for the students during lunch and before and after school.

Jason became seventeen and still chose not to drive; however, we were able to convince him to get his learner's permit, so he could practice. Jason continued to see a Department of Mental Health (DMH) counselor and psychiatrist to monitor his depression. The purpose of DMH is to provide "a full range of community and inpatient services to citizens of all ages who are emotionally disturbed or psychiatrically disabled."[7] He still took the lithium, which the medical staff at the Lodge prescribed when he was discharged. He really was doing very well. Jason still had fears and anxieties in stressful situations, such as completing his homework. He was so used to school and the structure it offered, that I could just imagine him walking on his toes down the halls with a small, smiling grin on his face. Jason still talked to himself and repeated what was said to him. Although he had friends in band class, no one ever called Jason or came to see him. I continuously hurt for him, watching him be alone in his room on the Fridays when there was no football game.

"Why couldn't someone befriend him?" I often thought. But maybe, Jason did not really want a friend.

I wanted to shout, "Step right up! Who will be my son's friend?" I imagined putting an ad in the paper just to see how many people would respond. I wanted to go to school and ask the teacher to get a child to be a mentor for Jason. I often contemplated these ideas because I felt so desperate to find a friend for him. However, he never seemed to act like he missed having friends. I wished he did. I think a friend would have helped him feel wanted and needed.

When Jason was seventeen, he said, "I wish I had a friend." When I suggested people he might like to befriend, he always had an excuse. "What do I say on the phone? The person I would like to have for my friend is already a doctor, so he cannot be my friend too," he said. We finally realized Jason did not know how to make a friend. He saw me as his mom, so he believed I was unable to be a friend too. Jason put people in categories, and they had to be in only one category. We had a problem getting him to understand that a person could be a friend and a teacher, or a friend and a dad. He listed the rules he had for a person to be his friend, and no one could be his friend unless they were only his friend and had no other role.

Oh, the tears I have cried! Many parents have shared with me in tears that they had no one even trying to be their child's friend. Asperger's Syndrome children struggle to belong with their peers. They struggle with how to relate to others. Picking up social cues is extremely difficult for them. How I longed for someone to call Jason and ask him to go somewhere with them or stop by to play with him. People said they liked him. But, they did not like him enough to think of him as a friend or to want to spend time with him.

Jason is so truthful and faithful to others. Unfortunately, a friend is not someone a mom can manufacture, so there are no answers.

When all the other kids were out playing or going off to play foot-ball games, he was home watching the Discovery Channel or spend-ing time with himself. What a lonely world it must be! Honestly, I'm sure it does not bother him as much as it bothers me. He truly wanted someone to be interested in what he was interested in. He desired a friend to share all the facts about math or computers or a friend who would enjoy speaking German with him. I was truly thankful that Jason was well and not as depressed as he was before his stay at the Lodge. He seemed happy and content as far as we could tell.

I believe our world needs a lot of help in getting people to reach out to be a friend in deed, especially to people who do not know how to reach out. If only people would take a chance, they might find a friend for life. Think about who you could reach out to befriend, maybe someone who has a child with no friend. I believe that we should reach out and take the first step.

Time went by quickly as we watched our children grow into adulthood. Jason was eighteen years old and in the eleventh grade. As in previous years, he adjusted to school life quite well. His math teacher was the same as in ninth grade, and he was excited to be in her class once again. Band was band, and Jason had his classroom and on-the-field responsibilities down pat. He liked math class so much because he knew his math. Students relied on him for advice in trigonometry class. He said he felt needed.

Then one day, the students were given a trigonometry "cheat sheet" by the teacher. Now, all the students could look up the answers on the sheet that for so long they had relied on Jason to provide. The students did not need Jason for many of the answers, so he said he was not really needed anymore. His grades began to slip, and he became less enthusiastic about his favorite subject, math. German students liked Jason because he was great at speaking the language. His eleventh grade teacher had given him the best student of the year award in German. He also was selected as vice president of the German club.

Jason was not getting lost as much because he took responsibility for letting me know where he was at all times. He rode to school with his brother, Luke, now, so the school bus was no longer an issue. During the Christmas concert, he was given a solo part in the band for the drummer boy. Yes, he was the drummer boy! He did a great job on percussion, and we were so proud of all his accomplishments. It was amazing to watch and see how far our son had come since his hospitalization at the Lodge. It was a time of celebration. We were relieved and thankful our son was doing so well.

The situation changed quickly in February when Jason became lethargic again. He quit caring about his classes and his homework. He just did not care anymore and said so. "I'm not needed. I'm not a man," he said, "like 'Pepe' in John Steinbeck's story, 'Flight'." According to the story, when a man was needed, he became a man. Until then, "Pepe" was called a "Peanut" by his mother. Jason thought he was a peanut because he felt like he was not needed, so he was not a man.

He withdrew once again socially. "When Jason became depressed," his therapist declared, "his capacity to make logical, rational judgments deteriorated. Also, his preoccupation with spirituality grew to the point where he found it easy to rationalize his failures to perform school assignments, attend classes, take his medication, and nourish himself properly. Simultaneously, he was finally beginning to recognize and discuss his significant deficits in social and job skills." He thought God had to tell him when to do everything. He told us that if God did not tell him to open up his book, then he wasn't supposed to do it. Jason also believed God was telling him to give his money away and not to take his medications. The unexpected happened in February and March of 1998 when he was once again hospitalized in a short-term psychiatric hospital in

Aiken. He asked to go to the hospital for help because he was "stressed out" and couldn't take it any more.

Life was like a roller coaster. John and I felt our emotions were constantly being tested. Our lives together were difficult, and yet, we often looked at each other and said, "Hang in there!" Hanging in there and praying were all we could do. We were helpless, and although we had been through this in the past, the present was not getting any easier. Luke was ready to graduate from high school, and Jason was struggling just to stay out of the hospital. We did not need anyone to tell us what to do. We just needed someone to just stand by us and be there for us. Joyce, our families and friends all diligently prayed for us. They all listened a lot and were not judgmental. Thank goodness, we had our insurance and Medicaid, or we would have been bankrupt by now! Jason received Medicaid and SSI from the government for his disability when he turned eighteen. Our emotions felt bankrupt each day as we watched our son go through trials. We did not have any strength left. All our hope and trust were in God to bring us through the storms of life. Oh, how we wanted the trials to end! We had to cling to our faith.

13

Finding a Home Again

After two weeks of inpatient care and four weeks of outpatient care, we were faced once again with finding an appropriate long-term facility for Jason to transition him into adulthood. His condition was deteriorating. John and I searched many nights on the internet and made numerous phone calls to try to find a place to transfer Jason. We found only one facility in the whole country that could be the proper environment, which met the criteria for Jason's immediate needs.

Our insurance company chose to provide all the funds for Jason to live at Mountain Top Inn in Vermont. Our up-front out-of-pocket costs totaled only $3,000. We were thankful that we were able to find an Adult Care Facility for which our insurance would pay the entire cost. On June 19, 1998 Jason was transferred to Mountain Top Inn. Jason and I flew to Vermont to admit him.

The Mountain Top Inn was located in a rural community. It was a ten bedroom, three story, Victorian style home surrounded by a small wooded area and located in the heart of town. Jason's depression was severe to psychotic. They put him on all types of medicines to bring him out. The biggest change we noticed in him was that he started to sleep in his clothes. Also, he would not let them cut his hair, so when I went to visit him two months later, he was in shambles. Although he had begun to feel more confident, he chose to neglect taking care of himself unless it was required of him. The hospital staff felt that Jason was just going through a faze of not wanting to have his hair cut or shaved. "Let freedom ring," you could say. I was concerned because I know that neglecting to take care of yourself is a sign of depression.

His greatest interest was German. A fellow patient spoke German fluently which helped Jason to feel at home. It took him time to begin feeling comfortable and safe around strangers. Fortunately he had become close to some of the staff and patients. Just as Jason was beginning to adjust he received word that he must go home.

There was no school at the Inn, so the goal was to assist Jason in obtaining his GED (Graduate Equivalency Diploma), so they could transition him to a local community college. After learning the rules of the house, Jason stabilized on his medicine, and his depression lifted. The next step was to allow him to live in an apartment on the grounds. In the apartments, the hospital staff would begin to teach him independent living skills more intensely. Jason never made it that far.

Although he was making good progress in Vermont, three-and-a-half months into treatment, our insurance company wrote to inform us that they believed Jason needed a less restrictive environment. All his caregivers agreed he should remain in a restricted environment providing the continuum of care and treatment intensity that he required. He did not deal well with change and needed the continued support of the care that the Inn offered. We appealed twice to no avail, so he was once again faced with an even more drastic change.

We felt numb and overwhelmed, knowing that we could no longer help him like he needed. The stress was too much for us to handle. We became angry at the system. The system said that a person could only remain in inpatient care for three months, and then he must return home. We wanted to contact our senators and try to make the insurance company pay to keep him where we felt he belonged. Jason needed more time to heal. He had just started making progress. How could we fight the system and win? We were so tired that we had to pick our battles, and this was one we were too weary to attempt.

When Jason left for Vermont, we packed up all of his clothes and belongings and shared with him that we felt it best that he not come home to live with us ever again, because his doctors felt it was time for him to live independently. My health was poor with all the stress. We knew that independence was critical in life, but especially so for an adult with a disability. We needed to give him the chance to separate from us. I knew in my heart I had to let him go once more. I needed to set him free to be himself. No matter how hard it would get, we felt that it was time for others to share the burden and care for our son. Jason was eighteen years old. We wrestled with the decision of how to tell Jason. We did not want him to feel more depressed, but rather to learn to trust others and himself for his care. When the Inn discharged Jason in November, I had to find an alternative home for Jason.

I quickly found a place near Macon, Georgia. I visited and liked what I saw. The home was situated on 50 acres of land. It had a commercial nursery that was kept by the residents and the staff who lived on the grounds. Most of the patients were mildly mentally challenged (MC), and a few were quite similar to Jason. They all struggled with social skills. It was a well-kept home with seven houses nicely spaced on the 50 acres of land. One building was used for administration, kitchen and chapel. The other six buildings were homes for the clients. Jason would have his own room with a private bathroom. In the middle of November, we transferred Jason to the home in Macon, Georgia.

They accepted his SSI (Social Security Income), but unfortunately, not his Medicaid. The State of Georgia had specific qualifications that a child must be mentally challenged with an IQ of 70 or lower to receive any Medicaid funding, and Jason's IQ was above average. We were faced with a $1,700 a month bill for him to remain in the home. The staff had informed us that Medicaid would cover his care, but they were very wrong. Jason was very unhappy at the home, and I knew it was time to somehow bring him back to live in South Carolina closer to home. Jason thought he was really mentally challenged, and you could tell he was confused about a lot of issues due to living in an environment where others seemed so different. Funny isn't it, that although Jason was different in many ways, he still knew what normal was!

14

Decisions, Decisions

The task began for me to transition Jason back to South Carolina from Georgia. I remember realizing one day that I could have a mentor live with Jason. Why couldn't I make up a plan for him? Jason could not help me because he still did not know what he wanted for his life. No matter what the issue was, decisions for him were very difficult throughout his life. I asked my husband, John, what he thought about me asking a college student to assist us if, in turn, we would give him free rent and utilities. John thought that was a good idea. So, I prayed diligently for someone who could help and asked God for guidance with all the details.

One Sunday morning at church, I saw a young man I had known since he was sixteen. Dave bowled with Jason on his bowling team. I knew Dave was now in college but living with his parents. Dave had a handicap due to a car wreck when he was a teenager. He was in a coma for three weeks and had to relearn how to walk and talk. So, I boldly asked Dave if he would consider my proposal. Dave was excited at the prospect, and quickly decided that he would love to live with Jason in an apartment that we selected. To bring Jason home to South Carolina meant to transfer his SSI and Medicaid in order to receive services from Department of Mental Health (DMH) and Department of Disabilities and Special Needs (DDSN). The South Carolina DDSN is a state agency that "plans, develops, coordinates and funds services within the state with the severe, lifelong disabilities of: mental retardation and related disabilities, autism, traumatic brain injury, spinal cord injury and similar disability."[8] Jason would enroll back in school at Jefferson High School for the winter semester.

I was so excited to watch Jason as we brought him home from Macon, Georgia, in early February. Dave and Jason had a two bedroom, two bath apartment. Jason would receive his $530 from SSI and food stamps to pay for the rent and utilities each month. John and I paid $250 a month for Dave's half of the rent. Dave went to the University of South Carolina at Aiken and applied at Tri-Development to work as Jason's mentor. Tri-development is a non-profit organization which provides residential, vocational and other community based support services to individuals with disabilities and special needs. Dave had to complete certification in order to be paid for working with Jason. So now, Dave not only had a place to live but also a part-time job helping Jason with independent living skills.

I was spending all my time getting Jason moved in and adjusted to his new apartment. The apartment was within walking distance of the local grocery store, several shopping centers, a bank, and restaurants. He still refused to drive. Dave took Jason grocery shopping once a week. He had not only Dave as a mentor but also a woman named Christy, who was his case manager from DMH. Christy taught Jason how to walk across the highway to the stores and how to use the Aiken pubic transportation. Dave practiced with him until Jason got it down pat. Now was the time for Jason to learn to make decisions on his own.

Throughout his life, Jason struggled with making the smallest of decisions. We could not get Jason to make a quick decision. Most big decisions had to be thought out and prayed about before being finalized. Jason was just so unsure of himself. The little decisions that needed to be made each day created fear inside of Jason. He feared the consequences of a poor decision. Whether it was buying shoes or eating a hamburger, every decision was important to him. Dave and Christy chose to work closely with him regarding decision making skills. The following is a picture of a typical visit to a restaurant: We decided to take Jason out to eat. We had to choose a restaurant that would be the best choice for him since he had such difficulty deciding what to eat. We couldn't go to one fast food restaurant because he was boycotting them for personal and spiritual reasons. So, we decided to try another fast food restaurant. We got in line, and while others were gathering behind us, Jason could not decide what to order. When he decided, he ordered like this, "I want a hamburger. Do you have wheat buns?" The cashier replied, "No sir." Jason responded with, "I do not want any bun, just meat, and no onion and just a little mustard and ketchup, but no mayonnaise. Oh, and I want a lemonade with just a little ice, and a little water in the bottom, with lemonade on top."

By the time we completed our family's order, we were sure that those behind us in line must be wondering what was going on with this kid. I wanted to turn around and say, "Please excuse us, but my son takes extra time to make his decisions and needs all of us to be patient, so please understand." John and I were sometimes angry and embarrassed because he was being so inconsiderate of others. Luke, our younger son, got embarrassed with all the questions Jason asked when ordering. John and I were also exhausted by how long he took with the smallest of orders. We had to consciously and continually make sure we remembered to assist him with preparation for eating out. Sometimes, it went so smoothly, but other times we had to interfere and assist him, so we could move along. His time frame was not the same as our family's time frame.

On Sunday, a day of rest, Jason would not eat out. He felt a strong conviction about it as he grew into adulthood. So, if we went out on a Sunday, we just brought him a sandwich so he could eat with us. If the restaurant was closed one day a week, to allow a day of rest for all the employees, then and only then, would he choose to eat at that restaurant on Sundays. The hardest part, was remembering that I could not purchase anything on Sunday or he would not eat it. One Sunday, I had to have milk, so I rushed to the store. On Friday of the same week, I noticed Jason eating his cereal with no milk and asked John why he was doing that. John replied, "Remember you bought the milk on Sunday?" I just forgot, but he could not allow any exceptions to his rules.

We did not always give in to his idiosyncrasies, but sometimes we had to weigh how important the situation was. We worked to avoid little confrontations and anxiety. Jason really believed in what he was doing. The things he could eat or not eat were important to him. The things he would not eat were white bread and any products that Jason saw contained MSG (Monosodium Glutamate).

As Jason began to live alone, he spent hours at the local grocery store analyzing product descriptions on the labels in order to know what products were healthy and edible, according to his rules. When he first moved to his apartment with his mentor, Dave, he spent four hours at the local grocery store. Jason made a list of products he could eat by reading all the labels carefully. He spent the time wandering the aisles and seemed suspicious to the manager. I found out later that the manager was going to have him arrested. Fortunately, someone recognized him and explained the situation. People in the community felt quite comfortable with Jason after they understood his special needs. They were quite helpful.

It would be good if we all stepped back and tried to see circumstances through Jason's eyes. He not only needed structure but help in learning how he was perceived by others, so others could understand him. As our son grew into adulthood, he made decisions more quickly and adjusted himself to others' expectations. It was important to take time to listen carefully to Jason when he spoke. Decisions were important to him, and he wanted to always do the right thing and make the right decisions.

I had to learn to trust his decisions, so I could move on. Letting Jason fall was not easy, especially when I knew he had special needs. No matter what, I had to let go, so Jason could learn how it felt to be independent. I needed to give him that chance not only for him but for myself! We were overwhelmed by stress at times and needed a rest. Thankfully, now was the time to let others help. I put together another plan, so a team of people could help our son.

For the first time ever, the State of South Carolina was providing resources for our son. It was significant to me that we had waited so long for our state to provide Jason with a structured home. Previously, we had to find all the resources ourselves, and then make them work for our son. I felt that the state should have assisted us in obtaining the resources. Perhaps they did their best to help us with the resources they had available and within the structure of their established system. We have grown stronger by struggling through this process. However, my concern was for those who didn't have the time and resources to get the care for their child. Jason was about to learn to become independent with all the resources we were putting in place.

15

Wrap Around Services

What I needed for Jason was a plan to help him to transition to adulthood. I had Dave as Jason's mentor and roommate and Christy as his case manager at Department of Mental Health (DMH). DMH, Department of Disabilities and Special Needs (DDSN), and the public schools agreed to meet with me and his psychiatrist to assess his current needs. I called it the round table, and I hoped for him to be the center of the discussion as we evaluated resources available to meet his needs.

During the meeting, I watched carefully as the staff from both public systems expressed their viewpoints and set goals for Jason. For some unknown reason, they did not come together as a team. I felt like I had to help them. So, I gave them the goals that I had prepared for transitioning him. I was convinced that Jason needed a mentor or tutor as soon as possible. I felt that the school district or DMH should be responsible to help pay for these services. I was discouraged when I saw that the areas of need were clearly defined, but no one seemed willing to allocate the money to meet the needs. Both systems always passed the buck to the other, and I wondered why money was always an issue that slowed our progress when it came to Jason's well-being. Such a small amount of money was needed for him to remain out of hospitals. The meeting ended with little resolved, but I was able to get DMH and DDSN to look at the goals for his future and to consider what type of services they could provide to meet those goals.

I was pleased to see all the agencies collaborating together and they agreed the needs were acute but they had no real answers for us. However, wrap around services were ordered for his care through DMH and DDSN. Wrap around services are specific services organized for an individual by the various agencies working together as one. Dave was being trained as a mentor. Christy began to work with Jason on independent living skills. A DMH counselor chose to meet with Jason each month to review his goals and keep a close eye on his depression and medications. DDSN provided the mentoring services and coordinated the services with Jefferson High School to make sure that Jason's IEP (Individualized Education Plan) was being carried out. Jason's resource teacher, Dr. Fulmer, assisted Jason in receiving Vocational Rehabilitation Services within the school setting.

Dr. Fulmer actually worked with Jason during the summer of 1999 to help Jason catch up on his English. He also assisted as Jason completed the English requirements for his senior year in high school. I was elated by all the support and assistance Jason was receiving. He took Jason to various colleges to let him get a feel for a transition in the near future. Jason was flourishing. He began to see that he could live on his own and make decisions on a daily basis. He had his own banking account right across the street from the apartments. Dave and Jason got along fine. Since Dave was working with Jason, he was getting paid for his mileage through the Tri-Development Center.

I was so amazed and thankful for the help God provided when Jason and Dave first moved into their apartment. Jason only had a bed and dresser to his name. People from our church sold them a TV and an entertainment center for a small price. We gave them an old couch and a washer and dryer. Dave's parents came and fixed up the kitchen nicely and made sure Dave had all that he needed. Their needs were amply met. I felt as if a huge burden had been lifted and that others were carrying the burden now.

Six months passed quickly and Jason and Dave's apartment now seemed so dark and small. I looked for a better home for them, and within a month we moved them to a new apartment complex. This apartment was on the same side of town but was much nicer. The apartment complex had a pool and tennis courts along with a weight room. It was just what I wanted because it was spacious and bright. They were moved in just before the beginning of Jason's senior year.

The time came for another IEP, and Jason wanted to complete his senior year as a partially homebound student. We purchased his books, and he chose to go to school for physics and math. Then he planned to go to the resource room for tutoring. This plan gave him the freedom to go home early. In the afternoon, Mr. Daly came by and worked on the remaining subjects and taught him history. The schedule seemed like a perfect situation. The faculty worked so hard and generously spent time meeting Jason's individual needs. They saw our need was great and made sure our needs were met. What a relief that was for us!

After about nine months, Dave and Jason began to have some communication problems. Jason resented being told what to do. Although Jason was nineteen now, he was emotionally about six-teen. It was hard for him, knowing that he was becoming an adult, but in some ways was still being treated like a child. How difficult that must have been for him. Jason just did not know what he wanted to do. This caused him confusion.

December of 1999 came, and Jason was beginning to struggle with school again. Dr. Daly could not get Jason to even put his name on tests he was administering. The school faculty and I became concerned. Jason was withdrawing, becoming more echolalic and obsessing about God. He believed that God was telling him to get rid of things from his apartment. Jason thought that God had to tell him everything he should do or he would not do it. Jason was in a manic state this time, yet was physically lethargic when it came to doing anything. Mania can be described as an "excitement of psychotic proportions manifested by mental and physical hyperactivity, disorganization of behavior, and elevation of mood. Other symptoms may include: being easily distracted, irritable, rageful, paranoid, and withdrawn."[9] John and I became deeply concerned. The school called an emergency IEP (Individualized Education Plan) meeting for January.

On Friday, January 7, 2000, I took our son to a psychiatric hospital in Augusta for possible admission. The administration refused to admit him. They agreed he was out of touch with reality, but that he was not suicidal or homicidal. Therefore, insurance would not pay. I was furious and afraid for my son's life. Jason was taking lithium and antidepressants, but I believed that he needed a change of medications or maybe an altering of dosage.

My hope was that Jason would not deteriorate any further. He was using God to protect him from making any decisions. Jason felt he had to get his homework perfect, so he would work on it over and over again. He was Obsessive Compulsive. He actually thought that God would open up his books for him. This was delusional thinking. We were exhausted to say the least.

Monday morning came, and Jason had his IEP meeting to attend. After much discussion, the team concluded that he needed hospitalization. Their greatest concern was his lack of interest in school. Jason stated that he did not know what to do, so the school gave him their final recommendation: 1) fill out the GED application and take the test on February 2, 2000 2) discontinue physics, but attend resource class for GED preparation 3) discontinue homebound instruction immediately. There were no words to describe the despair I was feeling that day. I had no control over what was happening to our son. I was lost.

The next day I took Jason to the Department of Mental Health (DMH) to see his counselor and psychiatrist. They were in agreement that Jason needed hospitalization. I didn't want to take the responsibility of committing Jason to the hospital, so I let the counselor sign the commitment papers. I was thinking about the future. I was concerned that Jason might blame me someday for putting him in the hospital. I could rest now, knowing Jason was in good hands, although deep down, I was weary and confused. I could not begin to understand what had happened to Jason.

He remained in the hospital in Augusta for 10 days. Then he went to a court hearing to decide whether he should go back to Augusta for further evaluation. John and I had to testify to a judge regarding his unwillingness to take medications and his need for extensive care. This was a painful experience for us. The judge agreed and sent Jason back to the hospital until he was willing to take his medications. The nurses never told Jason he had to take his medications. They just asked, so he didn't take them. I intervened, once again, and informed them that he would only take them if he was told that he must. They followed my advice, and the next day Jason cooperated by taking his medications.

Jason came home a week later and was placed back in his apartment with wrap around services. Dave was so glad Jason was doing better because he was afraid for him also. His lithium was increased. The doctors added other antidepressants to help with his major depression. The medications seemed to help. The doctors spoke with us concerning Jason's diagnosis. They concluded that Jason was showing signs of manic depression, also called bipolar disorder. The doctors were not willing to change the diagnosis for now. We needed to wait for future developments.

Jason decided not to go back to classes, but just study at the school for his GED. About two weeks later, he quit altogether and decided to go to the Adult Education Department to get his diploma through Jefferson High School. Here was a young man, who was so capable of completing his college preparatory classes, deciding to forgo his college prep diploma to get a high school certificate of achievement. He was so bright, and yet emotionally handicapped. Jason often blamed his medication on his performance. He said he could not do math anymore because the medicines caused him great difficulty concentrating. Maybe he was right, because he was on a variety of medications to control his multiple symptoms. The one thing he loved the most was math, and now he no longer had the desire to do it. His math skills were excellent. His SAT's came back in November of 1999 showing a total score of 1080. His math score alone was 670, which put him in the 95th percentile. This told us a lot about Jason and how gifted he truly was.

Jason had learned so much since living on his own with Dave. He ventured out to ride the city bus when needed. Jason did his own laundry, cleaned his apartment, and cooked on a regular basis. Dave helped him to structure his days, so they could be the most productive. Jason was still echolalic and Obsessive Compulsive, but with his medications, the symptoms were lessened. We were so proud of Jason and how far he had come. He graduated with a Jefferson High School Certificate through the Adult Education Department on June 7, 2000! What a milestone for all of us. We were so proud of what he had accomplished. When Jason was first diagnosed with depression, Asperger's Syndrome, ADD, and OCD the doctors all predicted he would probably never live on his own. I was so thankful for the large team of people who worked together to make our dream a reality. We believe our Lord pulled all the people together and gave us the vision to pray and persevere to move Jason toward independence. Our dreams became a reality. Our son had learned to live on his own!

16

I Can't Fix It

Jason got a job in November of 2000 at Chick-fil-A working in the dining room. He worked part-time about five to ten hours a week. We were so happy for him. His confidence rose dramatically. He enjoyed the job and really cared about the quality of his work. He still struggled with Obsessive Compulsive tendencies. Jason thought that he never got the dining room clean enough. He felt like he wasn't doing a good enough job. He continued to struggle with low self-esteem, which even being employed couldn't remedy.

Jason met a man at church named Bill and became very close to him. Bill was a young married Christian man. Bill wanted to help Jason to grow spiritually and to take more responsibility as a young man. After a few months of knowing each other, Jason and Bill came to us and asked if Jason could live with Bill's family. I was uncertain at first; however, after spending time with the family we decided it would be okay.

Jason's life changed, once again, in February from having a mentor in his apartment to living with friends. Jason was now twenty, and we wanted him to make decisions for himself. I had peace knowing Jason was well taken care of. Jason rented the upstairs room with his own bathroom for $250 per month. I gave him cash from his SSI (Social Security Income) check to pay his bills. Jason kept the monthly receipts for his food, clothing, and other expenses. As long as he did not get manic and give away all of his money he could take care of his own finances. The family was able to keep Jason responsible.

Jason lived with this family from February 2001 until May 2001. In that time period, Bill helped Jason buy a used moped and taught him to ride it. Here was our 6'1" son riding his moped on the streets of Aiken. He was so proud and independent. One day at Wal-Mart, he left the keys in his moped, and someone stole it. John and I quickly allowed him to purchase a new one for $100 a month. He could go whenever and wherever he wanted. This gave Jason a range of freedom and independence, which helped him to feel confident. Jason took good care of his moped. Smiles were often seen on his face.

Jason signed up for a German class 4 days a week at the University of South Carolina, Aiken. He continued to work at Chick-fil-A five to ten hours a week. Tri-Development through DDSN provided Jason with a job coach whose sole responsibility was to assist Jason in getting an extra ten hours of work. Bill wanted Jason to be financially independent. He thought it was a worthwhile goal for him to work towards getting off SSI. However, Jason needed the SSI in order to provide his Medicaid. If he went to the hospital, then my insurance would only cover a limited amount. Medicaid was my only protection from financial liability for his mental health care. He did get a Medicaid card every month that provided 4 prescription drugs free. Medicaid picked up all bills not paid by our insurance company. The Department of Mental Health in Aiken monitored Jason's medications and progress.

After over a year of waiting, Jason was selected for Section 8 housing which meant he could move into an apartment by himself. Jason felt he was unable to work more than ten hours a week and handle his class too. Bill wanted him to work 20 hours or move out. Jason chose to move out. He had his SSI and food stamps to take care of himself. Bill's family had been so good for Jason, but Jason was not ready to go the extra mile. I wish he had, but Jason had his own timing, and it was not ours or Bills.

All was well for a month or so in his new apartment. Jason passed his first German test but failed the second one. The unthinkable happened again. Jason became obsessed regarding the fear of prosecution by the IRS. He was worried that he would be accused of claiming too many or too few deductions on his employee W-4 forms. He said, "Is it legal to claim more than one exemption if you live alone?" What a question! So John and I embarked on explaining the W-4 form to Jason. That was a mistake! "Claiming more than you have is not telling the truth!" he proclaimed with such conviction. "How do we explain this to him, so he can understand and be willing to drop the subject?" we asked ourselves. Jason was questioning why he could claim more than one on his W-4 form when the government states that you can if you choose to want more exemptions deducted from your paycheck.

The phone rang in my kitchen late one morning. It was Jason telling me he failed his last German test. It was 11 a.m. He should have been in class, but no, he was at home calling the IRS about his taxes. You see how things had to be black or white, not grey or in between. He should have been in class earning a good grade since we gave him the college money as a Christmas present. I felt quite angry and frustrated over the whole matter, but Jason could not find peace of mind until he felt he had the right answer.

The obsession with taxes grew into depression. Jason failed his class for the semester. He was taking anti-abortion material and making posters to show on the street corners. He was becoming manic again. The depression and obsessions continued despite medication changes. Over the summer, Jason grew gradually worse. In June of 2001, he was in severe depression with psychosis and chose to return to the psychiatric hospital in Aiken. His lithium was tapered off, and he was placed on various medications. He remained in the hospital for suicidal ideation for three weeks. He returned to his apartment.

On August 27th, Jason returned to the hospital with suicidal thoughts. He called me up, and I could tell by the tone of his voice that something was the matter. Jason was crying and afraid. He was all alone in his apartment and did not know what to do. He said he had a knife and decided to put it down and call me. I knew he meant business. I frantically insisted that John get in his car and drive as quickly as possible to get him. Jason just talked to me the whole time and kept stopping at intervals to catch his breath. I told him to slow down and breathe deeply to keep his mind off of the knife and wait for his father to get there. I kept reminding him that John was almost there, so that he would not give up hope.

I was so afraid for our son. His life was in danger, and I could not do anything but hope and pray. My heart hurt with a longing to hold him like I did when he was a little child and tell him, "It's all right. Mom can fix it." I could not fix it this time. It seemed so easy when he was a child but, as an adult, the choices of life were up to him. There is no manual to help raise a child with Asperger's Syndrome and bi-polar disorder. John took Jason to the hospital that night and they placed him with a guard in the emergency room until they could transport him to the psychiatric facility across the street. He went into the hospital voluntarily. Even the doctor was beginning to get discouraged. His concern was Jason's lack of motivation to try to overcome failures in his school and job. His boss at the job took him off the payroll until he could return. But Jason chose not to return. He also chose not to complete or pass his classes. He was afraid of failure. How could we help him overcome his fear of failure? Medicines wouldn't do this. We believed that the power to master his fears had to come from within Jason.

The doctor felt strongly that Jason needed a group home more than a medication change. He had become a danger to himself, and the risk was substantial if he was left alone in the apartment. So, John and I once again searched for homes in our state that would be adequate for Jason. Where could we go to find a home?

17

Falling Through the Cracks

I have learned along the road of life that I had to teach faculty and administrators of the school system, my neighbors, and my family about Asperger's Syndrome and bipolar disorder. There wasn't a manual that taught me how to deal with Asperger's or autism. The children are all so different, and no one knows how children are born with autism. It was up to John and me to get what was needed to serve Jason's best interest. He needed a non-violent atmosphere with young adults, preferably his age, who had similar disabilities. Living with a mentally challenged young adult was not an option based on our past experiences at the home in Macon, GA. Our state did not have any homes available that could even be considered.

If Jason had alcohol problems or drug issues, then there would be a home for him. If he wasn't taking medications, then there might be a home for him. If he was mentally challenged, then there definitely would be a home. If, if, if...The road was long and all uphill. Even with us on the front lines fighting for what Jason needed educationally, socially, emotionally and physically, he was still falling through the cracks. I just thought once high school was over, we could rest because Jason would go off to college or attend our community college where he would definitely find peers with similar interests.

No, that did not happen. Jason's confidence, motivation and determination went out the window once he was hospitalized from the stress related to college. There are colleges that will work specifically with Asperger's Syndrome children in other states, but not in our state. The cracks are too big and too many! These colleges sound great, but not at the cost of $58,000 a year! Middle income families like we are cannot afford the cost. Once again, we were forced to prayerfully work out with him a program for success. Since he was afraid of failure, he would not go to school or work.

We chose to keep him in his apartment with wrap around services until we could find a place for him. We had no choice. There was no place for Jason. The Department of Mental Health kept a close eye on him, and so did we. I was worried, but what could we do? Where could we go? September came, and Jason's condition remained unstable. He became obsessed and manic again, and thought God had to tell him every move he should make. He believed medications were evil and that he should not be taking them. We begged him not to quit his medications, but he began to taper them off. We found ourselves in his mental health counselor's office asking for intervention. They agreed to hospitalize him. Since Jason would not go on his own, the counselor signed him over to a psychiatric hospital in Columbia, S.C. I was devastated and worn out physically and emotionally. I needed a rest. Since I suffer from bipolar disorder too, it was hard to watch him suffer. We knew a little about what he was going through and hoped the best for him. I just wanted my son alive and well, and I would do anything to make him well. It just wasn't in my power.

Sometimes I felt as if I could hardly breathe. I felt desperate amidst the day. I wanted to go inside my bedroom and cry out to God to make it alright. I didn't know what was wrong except that I felt down and helpless. I was helpless to help Jason. I kept trying, and I just couldn't understand why I just didn't give up. He was depressed and continually reminded me with his metaphoric speech. He would use words or an image to explain what he really meant when he was depressed. I could not do or say anything right, and when I tried to make it right, it was all wrong. I had to let Jason fall. I could not make my son happy. He had to do that for himself. We could not talk to Jason because it felt like he was not listening. All I could do was pray and try hard not to confront Jason with words, which had no meaning to him.

I was so desperate, but no one could help me but God. I had to give him to God, because I did not have the answers. Abraham took his son, Isaac, up to Mount Moriah to sacrifice him. Abraham did not know why God commanded him to do such a thing. He just knew that he had to do what God told him to do. So, Abraham obeyed God. God chose to give Abraham a ram to sacrifice as soon as he saw how obedient Abraham was. I had to follow Abraham's example and offer my son to Him for His purposes.

All of our children are a gift from God, and we should give them all back to God sometime in life. The key for me was to accept what could not change which was Jason's condition and the circumstances around him. God had to do the changing. Despite all the difficult days, we should go to bed each night and be at peace that we did our best. The rest was up to our great God! God made our children just the way they are to give back to the world something of value. They are so special.

Jason was committed in the state mental hospital in Colombia for ten days. Then, he was brought before the courts for release. We shared with the judge that he needed a group home, and that it was not wise for him to go back to his apartment. We asked him to keep Jason in the hospital until the staff could help us find an appropriate placement for our son. The judge agreed. Soon, we got a phone call from the hospital in Columbia. The social worker had found a home for Jason in a residential senior living apartment complex.

They took various ages with various physical disabilities. We went to look at the apartment and liked it a lot. They offered rent and utilities with one meal a day for $900 a month. They also took over the responsibility of his medications. Jason only had $550 with SSI.

I began to search for ways to fund the apartment. We contacted our Senators, Department of Mental Health (DMH), and Department of Disabilities and Special Needs DDSN) asking for assistance for Jason. We explained that the cost of the apartment was less than the cost of placing Jason in a group home setting. We even contacted the Ombudsman Office of the Governor of South Carolina asking for assistance. Within days DMH and DDSN agreed to share the cost of Jason's rent by providing $250 a month each. His old moped wore out at 5,000 miles, so he had to purchase a new one. He began to pay $25 a week as a payment. That left him with $125 per month for food, clothing and extras.

Jason moved into his apartment in the senior living apartment complex. His medications had stabilized. During the day, he needed some place to go until he chose to go to school or go to work. He was sleeping all day, and that was not allowed at the apartment. DMH put him in Bridges, a clubhouse to foster mental health for adults that need assistance in the daytime. He went there from 8 a.m. until 2 p.m. every day Monday through Friday. Jason found a church that he liked a lot and attended four times a week. On Thursday, they had Centrifuge, a young adult bible study that he liked. On Saturday, he attended a prayer meeting. On Tuesday evening he went to Aikido, a form of martial arts, with a friend he met named Tom.

So Jason had his days structured pretty well and liked the city. The senior retirement home made sure that he took his medications correctly and provided one meal a day. He got around on his moped and had the freedom to come and go as he pleased. The means of helping Jason function included financial support, the state resources, and his health care support. My husband, John dispersed his SSI check and the funds given by DMH and DDSN for his rent. Then, there were Jason's state resources. DMH consisted of his psychiatrist, whom he saw every other month, and his counselor, whom he saw every month. DDSN provided a case manager, who evaluated his Person Centered Plan and made sure that his caseworker followed the plans, goals, and objectives for the fiscal year. Jason and his case manager designed his Person Centered Plan, which detailed what he wanted to do with his life and how that would be accomplished. Our private health insurance company and Medicaid met his health care needs. So, his case was carefully organized and funded (see diagram).

Jason decided to go to Vocational Rehabilitation each day from Bridges. He took the city bus from Bridges to Vocational Rehabilitation then back to Bridges. He went faithfully for about six months and then quit. He got bored and said they didn't have anything else for him to do. He knew he could do better than just a conveyer belt job where he sat around doing the same thing over and over again. He realized that he was unwilling to get just any job. He wanted one in his area of interest, computer networking. He truly was trying, but not as much as everyone wanted him to. We explained to him that after a person does a job well, then they get better jobs. Everyone has to start at the bottom. Jason just could not seem to understand that he wasn't qualified to get the job he wanted. He knew what he wanted, but his expectations were unrealistic.

What a blessing to have Jason living just 40 miles from home, on his own and loving it! If he needed us, we were nearby. Yet he was far enough away from home that he could lead his own life. As he continued to live independently, Jason would have to wait for either a change in himself or a change in the system. We think that it would be beneficial to our state to give the mentally ill the opportunity to live healthier lives if Vocational Rehabilitation would open its doors wider to collaborate with the Department of Mental Health. Together, they could explore options in the work force or in furthering the education of the mentally ill. Jason still needs specialists who work with Asperger's Syndrome often in order to get the right assistance.

I know I am only dreaming, but, oh, how I wish we could have filled in some of these cracks for his sake and ours. Jason and other Asperger's Syndrome children can give so much to our lives, and to the world if and only if, we reach out and help them to be a part of our world.

Independent Support System for Jason

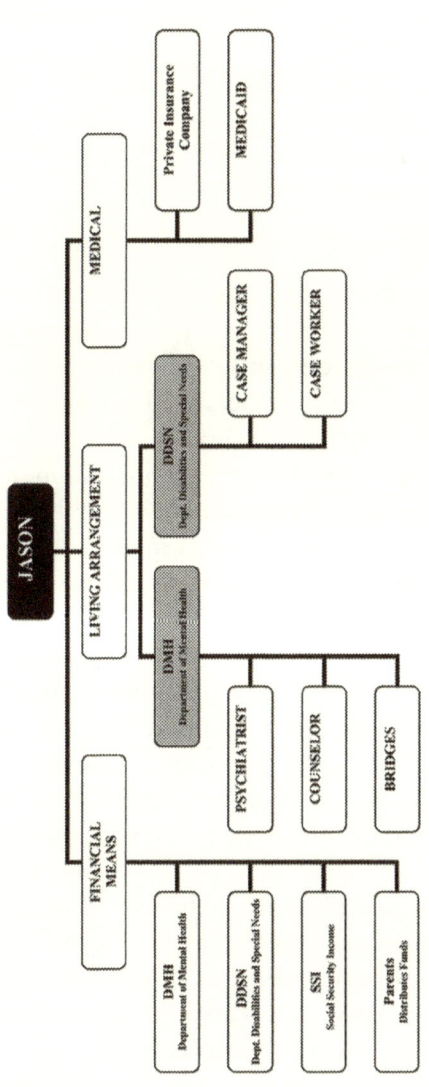

18

Present Day

Now, we are at a crossroads. Jason has learned to live independently so well, but he still refuses to get a job or go to work. Each day he faithfully goes to Bridges and waits and waits for something to change. Resources are needed to assist him in developing his vocational skills, but they are not available at this time. I believe he doesn't want to get a job. Getting a job would mean extra expectations that he would have to meet. He is afraid that more expectations will be placed on him. He has expressed that he wants to take small steps carefully, so that he will not become depressed. We have to accept Jason's timetable. He is a scared little boy living inside a young man's body and learning how to become a man. I can see in his eyes that he wants to make it on his own. Also, he has begun to gain confidence. This shows in his smiles and carefree attitude. Jason is now 24 and goes to a church where people accept and befriend him. Jason calls them his friends. What a miracle! What peace and joy to know that my son has made friends. After 20 years of prayers and tears, my son says he has a friend his own age!

Jason says he goes to church to be around people. He says he is good at obtaining, processing, distributing information. He can obtain and process information, but I wonder if anyone will want what he has to distribute. He is afraid that no one will want to hear about it. He connects with someone when they have something intellectual in common. He forces himself to be with people to learn their niches and interests. He now has friends that he calls up just to talk or visit and to play video games. He has grown to be a very responsible, mature adult in some ways, but emotionally he is about eighteen. He lives a quiet life in his apartment by himself and loves it. I am so proud of our son and what he has accomplished. I pray daily that the world will know him, and he will know the world.

The qualities I have enjoyed the most about Jason are his wonderful uncanny sense of humor and his kindness and gentleness towards others. I like his dedication to obeying rules no matter what the consequences. I derive great satisfaction from watching him walk on his toes with such confidence when he is happy. Oh, how I love his creativity and his desire to do things just right. He has a love for learning new information. Our son hungers and thirsts after righteousness and has a heart for God. He is a fine son and a trustworthy young man. Despite all of the obstacles he faces, Jason has a meaningful life. I hope you will look for positive qualities in your child and be aware of his potential in life.

The excitement continues each day as we watch Jason grow into a man. I have let him go, and now I live a life of my own. It is scary not knowing how to help him and letting him make his own decisions. Strength comes each day that I realize it is not my job to make my son happy. The most important thing for me to share with you is that our children may not be what we want them to be according to the world's time table and expectations, but God created them and loves them just the way they are. If our children go to school, get a job, and learn to live independently, it will be when they choose to do so. What joy there will be when we watch them walk through life being what they have chosen to be and feeling at peace in the world they have chosen for themselves.

Epilogue

Many people were willing to work with us, such as physicians, hospital staff, teachers, and the state agency staff. Sometimes, their way was not our way. We often had to pick up the pieces and find a home for Jason. We knew there were services out there for Jason. The problem was how to access them. Many times those with Asperger's Syndrome do not fit into the category of people for whom resources are available. I believe we need to stand up and work using all the creativity that we have to make those resources fit our children. The staff of the state agencies all counted on us for direction and guidance to know how to meet Jason's needs. Our energy levels were constantly drained by the so called "system." Fortunately, our hopes overcame their doubts.

The insurance company continued to stand by us despite our differences of opinion. However, the company did not always work in Jason's best interest. We felt he needed to live at the Lodge for at least another year, but the company would not help us financially to make that happen. The frustration of having the company make a decision and then, within months, inform us that it would not pay for his care in Vermont was absurd. The company did not look at Jason and his needs but only at what meeting his needs would cost them. Thank goodness we had Medicaid. When our insurance did not cover a bill, Medicaid picked it up. The only thing Medicaid did not pay for was when our son was in Colorado and Vermont where our Medicaid was not accepted. God always provided the rest of the money through private resources.

It is important to me for you to know that John and I have been married for 26 years. Our struggles together have made us stronger. At first, John had difficulty accepting Jason's diagnosis. All those years of wondering what was wrong with our child, and then, when we finally found out, he went into denial. We often asked ourselves the questions, "What could we have done to prevent this from happening?" or "What could we do now to change this?" When all along, there was nothing that we could have said or done to change what happened in our lives. We found ourselves holding onto each other in tears many times, hoping and praying for a brighter future for our son. We chose not to give in to the doubts of others but to cling to each other. We never allowed ourselves to blame the other one for what was wrong with Jason. Our prayers were always answered—sometimes not as we had planned or hoped. Even now, we know that God has more answers for us. A marriage can survive torrents of despair only if there is hope. Hope that comes from God is real hope.

There were times that the "system" was not there for us. All three of us suffered because of it. I believe that the world needs not only to know what Asperger's Syndrome and bipolar disorder are but also to reach out and accept those affected. It is easy to see a broken bone or physical scars and sense the pain, but what about emotional or mental pain? We cannot touch it or see it, but it still causes pain. It is my hope that all of us will come one step closer to losing our fear of the unknown.

The school administration assumed Jason would go to college. I have learned that it is best not to assume anything about the future of your child, but to offer your child all the resources available, and let the child make choices as he gets older. At the age of fourteen, all states are mandated to provide Vocational Rehabilitation Services. Allow your child to experiment with these services. That way you won't be putting your child in a box that does not fit him/her. Each child has different symptoms of Asperger's Syndrome and bipolar disorder, so be very creative with your resources.

The support of others is so critical. John and I often found comfort through having our families just listen to us, and then physically help us when times were difficult. It has been hard for me to find the support I need. I continually make myself reach out, but sometimes no one can help but God. There is so much confusion about the symptoms of Asperger's Syndrome child in comparison to a typical child. I struggle daily trying to decide what behavior is Jason and what behavior is Asperger's Syndrome or bipolar disorder. I also suffer watching him struggle with bipolar disorder when I see so many of the symptoms in my own life. I don't want him to suffer with bipolar like I have. I have been hospitalized about twelve times over the time that this book spans. I have spent a lot of time teaching Jason that it is not what you have that is important, but it is what you do with what you have.

One of the many questions I have been asked over the years is, "Do you believe Jason can be healed? I always answer, "Yes I do." I believe Jason's life is a blessing from God, and God does not make mistakes. There is a Scripture that has always given me comfort when others ask "Do you think you did something wrong to cause this to happen?" I turn to the story in John 9: 3 where a man was blind since birth. Jesus answered, "It was neither that this man sinned, nor his parents; but it was in order that the works of God might be displayed in him." I also know that since Jason was not diagnosed until he was twelve years old, there are many years I could regret because I think I would have treated him differently. I do not allow myself to dwell on what could have been for Jason's sake. I accept the past as the time period when I did the best I could under the circumstances, and no one is to blame. I am comforted by the many Scriptures in the Bible that speak about God caring about his creation and how special each and every one of us is to Him. Psalm

139:13 says, "For Thou didst form my inward parts: Thou didst weave me in my mother's womb." You may be assured that God truly knows what you are going through. He will give you comfort for "God comforts the depressed…" 2 Corinthians 7:6. He will give you the strength also to get through anything that comes before you. 1 Peter 5:10 says, "And after you have suffered for a little while, the God of all grace, who called you to his eternal glory in Christ, will Himself perfect, confirm, strengthen and establish you." God loves us all and does not judge us. According to John 3:16, "For God so loved the world, that He gave His only begotten Son, that whoever believes in Him should not perish, but have eternal life. For God did not send the Son into the world to judge the world, but that the world should be saved through him." I hope this helps you to look to Him and find comfort through His Word. I have shared this with you to let you know how much I care for you.

Lastly, I hope what I have shared will make an impact on your life. I desire that you will choose as I have "to let go" when you believe it is the right time. There are children who will never be able to live on their own no matter how hard we try. However, with most children, it is still possible to give them the freedom and independence to make some decisions on their own and to fall down and pick themselves up whenever they have the ability to do so. Letting go of Jason has been the hardest thing for me to do. My prayer is that this book will make it easier for you to let go of your child no matter what he has been given in life. The journey continues for all of us.

References

1. The American Medical Association Family Medical Guide. Random House Inc., New York, 1987.

2. http://www.britannica.com. "Attention Deficit/Hyperactivity Disorder." September 28, 2004.

3. http://www.m-w.com. "depression" September 29, 2004.

4. Asperger Syndrome, Klin, Volkmar, Sparrow, New York, 2000.

5. The American Medical Association Family Medical Guide. Random House Inc., New York, 1987.

6. http.www.autism.org/si.html. Sensory Integrative, May 5, 2004. Cindy Hatch-Rasmussen, M.A., OTR/L

7. 2004–2005 Practical Guide To Services, South Carolina Department of Disabilities and Special Needs, Columbia, 2004.

8. 2004–2005 Practical Guide To Services, South Carolina Department of Disabilities and Special Needs, Columbia, 2004.

9. http://www.m-w.com. "mania." October 10,2004

Suggested Resources

"Asperger's Syndrome" a Guide for Parents and Professionals by Tony Attwood.

http://www.udel/bkirby/asperger—Online Asperger Syndrome Information and Support.

http://www.autism-society.org—Autism Society of America

0-595-34213-2

www.ingramcontent.com/pod-product-compliance
Lightning Source LLC
Chambersburg PA
CBHW020313290526
45784CB00003B/1495